God's
Remarkable Plan For Man

A Tree Of Life For Those Who Find It

Mary Adams

WESTBOW
PRESS
A DIVISION OF THOMAS NELSON

Scripture Source:
All scriptures used in this text are from the King James Version of the Bible.
The Author has taken the liberty to use bold lettering in some of the scripture texts to call attention to important key words to reveal meanings that may otherwise be overlooked—(bold-italic lettering and underlining in the scripture texts are supplied by the Author for emphasis).

Cover Image: by Wantha Ann Deaton
Art work on Poems: Adrift, Small Feet and Perfect Love by Wantha Ann Deaton.

WestBow Press books may be ordered through booksellers or by contacting:

WestBow Press
A Division of Thomas Nelson
1663 Liberty Drive
Bloomington, IN 47403
www.westbowpress.com
1-(866) 928-1240

ISBN: 978-1-4497-5548-5 (sc)
ISBN: 978-1-4497-5549-2 (hc)
ISBN: 978-1-4497-5547-8 (e)

Library of Congress Control Number: 2012910729

Printed in the United States of America

WestBow Press rev. date: 5/17/2013

I dedicate this book to my beloved friend Jane Carpenter Stephens (1944-1996). A more faithful and devoted friend could not be found. A truly gifted poet—her poems—like beautiful songs should be heard. I am pleased to have this opportunity to honor her by sharing some of the poems that were birthed from her beautiful soul.

Heart Song

Take dear Lord my merest songs,
For unto you they all belong.
And out from you they ever flow,
And out from you they each shall go.

Give me life-producing words,
Gentle heart songs that when heard,
Bring your peace like Noah's dove,
Created simply by your love.

Note: Part I of this book was written before the thought occurred, to include the poems. They fit so perfectly with the text it only took two hours to insert them in their proper place—as if the book was written to contain them—like fitting pieces into a puzzle that would be incomplete without them. Some of the poems in the text were written by Jane Stephens—some by Mary Adams others co-authored by both. As the book has expanded other poems have been written and included by the author in addition to the ones originally inserted.

Contents

Part II

Poem: Draw Me On

Foreword

I consider Mary Adams, to be a very humble young Lady. At the turn of the clock on her next birthday, chronologically, she will be seventy-two years young.

As the Holy Spirit has directed her pen, it is quite evident that the gift of knowledge and wisdom is producing understanding through the Word. Led by the Holy Spirit in her writing, Mary leaves self out of the equation, giving all the glory and honor to the Father, Son and the Holy Spirit; not appropriating to herself, what has been freely given by the Holy Spirit.

Mary is quite bold and adventuresome, through this divine heavenly gift, as she shares concepts that will challenge you to search deeper and deeper into the Word. At first reading, you will be stunned, amazed and burning with a desire to grab your Bible to explore and confirm her words; as I myself had to do, with much prayer, seeking confirmation from the Holy Spirit, whose mission is to lead us into all truth.

I was astounded, even after being in the ministry for sixty plus years, at some of the revelation and insight she presented. I had to withdraw a number of times from the reading to seek the Lord for verification. We are instructed to try the spirits and see if they are of God. This is a wise course to follow when presented with truth, beyond our present understanding.

When Mary honored me with the opportunity of writing this forward for her book, I went into intensive prayer and supplication, seeking guidance from the Holy Spirit. I wanted to be sure that I could be in complete agreement concerning the authenticity of what was being declared in the book before I could endorse and recommend it.

I went through a process to come to the place where I can wholeheartedly recommend and endorse this book. Rest assured that after reading this fabulous writing, the understanding of your heart will be transformed by the renewing of your mind.

You will find this book to contain an explosion of truth, expounding on the true work and function of the Holy Spirit among us. This book is a *must read* for every Christian and should be in the hands of every seminary student as well as professors and theologians.

Pastor Jimmy Sowder

Pastor Jimmy and Carol Sowder, at the time of this writing, are serving as missionaries in Costa Rica. He has been serving the Lord in ministry for more than sixty years. On his birthday Sept. 1, 2012, he will be ninety years on this earth. He is a prolific soul winner and continues his very effective witness every day. He has ministered in forty of the fifty states, including Alaska and Hawaii, as well as in thirty seven foreign countries. He has led eighteen Crusades and Holy Land tours through Israel; conducted ten Crusades in Northern Ireland. And twelve Crusades in Haiti. Directed Evangelistic Crusades in South Africa and Belgium—in the place now known as the Democratic Republic of Congo. He continues his very effective ministry of preaching, teaching, counseling and soul winning. His love and familiarity with the Word of God has prompted some to refer to him as a walking Bible—a true assessment— just mention a scripture text, and he can quote the chapter and verse where it can be found.

Adrift

Like a small boat adrift
   On a vast, rolling sea
Is my soul, set afloat,
   Lord, in thee.
And I'll rise or I'll fall –
   Peaceful skies, noisy squall
On the waves of the water
   That is thee.
And no terror shall o'er take me
   Nor winter's gale break me
When I rest in the waters
   Of the sea;
For the waves, as they roll,
   Never break love's control
And I'll rise or I'll fall,
   Lord, in thee.

May the Holy Spirit overshadow you and quicken the Seed of the Image of God that dwells within you. I pray for the Living Word to arise and confirm, bearing witness to the Word of Truth written within the pages of this book.

The Author

Introduction

This book was written especially for those who desire more insight into the Image of God; it presents a unique perspective of God's purpose and plan for mankind. God's Word is His witness and every concept of His Word must be verified, by His Word. "In the mouth of two or three witnesses shall every word be established" (II Cor. 13:1).

In order to fully understand the subject matter in this book, it would be beneficial for the reader to be familiar with the book of Genesis, particularly the story of creation, as well as being able to follow each generation and the significance of their lives, in unveiling the hidden treasure concealed within their contributions to the revelation and subsequent manifestation of Jesus Christ.

"Whom shall He teach knowledge and whom shall He make to understand doctrine? To whom He said, this is the rest wherewith ye may cause the weary to rest; yet *they would not hear*... But the Word of the Lord was unto them precept upon precept... line upon line; here a little, *and* there a little that they might go, and *fall backward and be broken and snared, and taken.* Wherefore hear the Word of the Lord, ye scornful men that rule this people" (Is. 28: 9-14). This is a scripture that has been widely misinterpreted as a positive word to follow, when it is clearly presented as a negative element to avoid; *declaring that they would not hear,* which resulted in their receiving the Word precept upon precept—here a little and there a little—*causing them to fall backward and be broken and snared and taken.* Rather than it being an instruction for them to follow, they are in fact being reprimanded for this particularly methodology.

God is displeased with the people for their lack of vision. "For the Lord hath poured out upon you the spirit of deep sleep, and hath closed your eyes... And **the vision of all,** is become to you as the words of a book that is sealed, which *men* deliver to one that is learned, saying, Read this, I pray thee: and he saith, I cannot; for it *is* sealed: And the book is delivered to him that is not learned, saying, Read this, I pray thee: and he saith, I am not learned. Wherefore the Lord said, Forasmuch as this people draw near *me* with their mouth, and with their lips do honor me, but have removed their heart far from me, and their fear toward me is taught by the **precepts of men**, Therefore, behold, I will proceed to do a marvelous work among this people, *even* a marvelous work and a wonder: for the wisdom of their wise *men* shall perish and the understanding of their prudent men shall be hid" (Is. 29:10-14). Since the varied interpretations of the Word are numerous and none are exactly the same—in order to see the Word in its continuity: **the vision of all**, rather than in precepts and lines, here a little and there a little—it is necessary that we give up our preconceived ideas and *allow the Holy Spirit to connect the dots from Genesis to Revelation.*

We are living in the dispensation of the Holy Spirit. "Nevertheless I tell you the truth; it is expedient for you that I go away: for if I go not away, the Comforter will not come unto you; but if I depart, I will send Him unto you" (John 16:7).

Before the day of Pentecost; Jesus appeared to His disciples and breathed upon them saying: "Peace be unto you: as my Father hath sent me, even so send I you. And when He had said this, He breathed on them, and saith unto them, Receive ye the Holy Ghost..." (John 20:21). When He breathed upon them they received the Holy Spirit to be *with them*, a covenant between Him and His disciples, preparing the way for the day of Pentecost—when they received the Holy Spirit to *dwell within them*.

On the day of Pentecost, the Holy Spirit appeared to those, who in one accord were waiting in an upper room for the Comforter to appear. Their obedience in waiting as they had been instructed was a sufficient show of their faith for the Holy Spirit to appear. "And when the day of Pentecost was fully come, they were all with one accord in one place. And suddenly their came a sound from heaven as of a rushing mighty wind, and filled the house where they were sitting" (Acts 2:1.2). The rushing mighty wind was the breath of God breathing upon them in the resurrection power of the Holy Spirit. The price for atonement had been paid, releasing the Holy Spirit to dwell among men.

The Holy Spirit is bringing to birth a new creation, in the Image of God, by a sin devouring—cleansing fire. God sent His Son, born of a woman, for the redemption of mankind. Jesus sent the Holy Spirit to reproduce in us His selfsame Image—the Image of God. Adam was *created* then *formed*—Jesus was *begotten*, and we are to be *transformed* into His likeness.

"Verily, verily, I say unto you, except a corn of wheat fall into the ground and die, it abideth alone: but if it die, it bringeth forth much fruit" (John 12:24). Jesus: the Seed of God is the corn of wheat that was planted, to reproduce after *His own kind,* as it was with all things that were created from the beginning. "Whose *seed* was in itself after His kind" (Gen. 1:12). *The Seed of His Image was planted in man at the beginning* of creation, and through the working of the Holy Spirit *we are to become Living Testaments.* The Old Testament reveals a God of *correction* through *judgment:* the *Father*—The New Testament reveals a God of *redemption* through *grace:* the *Son*—The Living Testament is being revealed, as the Word of God is written in our hearts, bringing forth *much fruit* and revealing God's *love* through mercy: The *Holy Spirit.*

Chapter One

Insight into His Image

Man has explored virtually every inch of planet earth, and through the eyes of the Hubble telescope in *outer space,* we have seen awesome sights light years away into the universe. However, there remains another territory that has yet to be fully explored: the *inner space* within man.

The purpose of this writing is to venture into this *veiled* territory, to explore the center of the universe *in* man—how we came into being—how we are wonderfully made in the Image of God—for what purpose and to what end, and to declare the end from the beginning. "Remember the former things of old: for I am God and *there is* none else; I am God and *there is* none like me, Declaring the end from the beginning, and from ancient times the *things,* that are not *yet* done, saying, My counsel *shall stand,* and I will do all my pleasure" (Is. 46:9.10). Alpha and Omega too—this is a universe that can only be explored from the inside out.

The Old Testament contains types and shadows of truth concealed, as well as vast hidden treasure. "And in that day

1

shall the deaf hear the words of the book and the eyes of the blind shall see out of obscurity and out of darkness" [when the light of truth illuminates the darkness] (Is. 29:18). The New Testament bears witness and gives expression to the truth as it is unveiled, illuminating us from within by the dawning of truth. As a flower blooms and its wonders unfold—may our souls unfurl with truth *unveiled* and blossom with understanding.

> The Spirit and the Word always agree,
> Yet—with limited vision—we are unable to see.
> The vast hidden treasure concealed therein.
> Seeing through a glass darkly—now unveiled,
> As understanding increases, illuminated from within.
>
> With the dawning of Truth, we comprehend,
> The Word of Truth—ever expanding,
> Never ceases to outdistance our finite understanding.
> Its height, depth and breadth, we can never outgrow,
> It is only when we are known—then we will know.

To fully comprehend the message in this book, one must first understand that the *hidden treasure* being *referred to*, concealed within the pages of the Old Testament, is not being limited to the literal historical, real events and people, but is being presented in the spirit of prophecy as well as in parables of types and shadows.

The Word of God has many facets and levels to convey, containing ongoing and unending revelation. It is a complete handbook with all of the revelation needed for the Holy Spirit— with our permission and cooperation—to revive the dormant

Seed of God's original creation within us—and in the world around us, completing His remarkable plan for man.

Jesus, the Express Image of His Father, spoke in parables; He, being the expression of His Father, is an indicator of His Fathers methods. There is much to be gleaned when viewed in this manner. As Boaz did for Ruth, God has left us some "handfuls of purpose" (Ruth 2:16), to be gleaned from the field of His Word that are less obvious gleanings—left behind after a bountiful harvest has been gathered.

"In the beginning God created the heavens and the earth" (Gen. 1:1). God was all in one, containing all of creation within Himself. He created the heavens and the earth by speaking them into existence, "Let there be," and there was. In Genesis chapter one He gave birth to His creation through His spoken word; it is an account of the creation of all things spoken into existence—the creation of the essence of life—*yet* without form. "Through faith we understand that the worlds were framed by the Word of God, so that things which are seen were not made of things which do appear" (Heb. 11:3). All things that now appear and are visible, were made from the invisible things of creation, before their formation. All that remains to be discovered is pre-existing and waiting to be revealed.

"In the beginning was the Word, and the Word was with God, and the *Word was God*" (John 1:1). Genesis chapter one is a description of the creation of all things, *spoken* into existence—*an invisible creation*. Chapter two describes the *forming* of the *visible creation*. "All things were made by Him; and without Him was not anything made that was made" (John 1:3). He is *omnipotent*: containing all power, *omniscient*: having infinite knowledge and *omnipresent*: present in all places at the same time—through His Seed that dwells in man. He is within us and all around us. God was never alone, because He contained all things within Himself—not willing to remain *all* in one, desiring to become all in all, He spoke into existence and then formed His masterpiece: Man.

Made in His Image

"And God said, let *us* make man in *our image, after our likeness…* So God *created* man in His *own* image in the Image of God *created* He him; *male* and *female* created He *them*" (Gen. 1:26.27). God is Spirit—being made in His Image and likeness they became Spirit beings. God's Image is clearly presented as male and female—the pattern in heaven for His creation on earth. This can be seen as invariable in the whole of creation— it takes male and female to reproduce after their own kind, not only mankind but the birds and the bees and the flowers and the trees; witnessing to the pattern of *male* and *female* for all of creation.

The Spirit body described in Genesis the first chapter cannot be altered by the body formed in Genesis chapter two. When a person loses a limb and feels phantom sensations in what no longer exists as a part of the visible body, it could be, because the Spirit body remains unchanged. Healing that occurs in the physical body, whether natural or supernatural, is generated in the Spirit body. We have a body within a body— an *incorruptible* body, unfettered with all parts intact—within a corruptible body.

The creation of Adam and Eve in the Image of God was before Adam was formed from the dust of the ground into the visible form of man. The forming of man was the manifestation of what had previously been spoken into existence in the unseen realm of the Spirit. "And the Lord God *formed* man *of* the dust of the ground, and breathed into his nostrils the breath of life; and *man* **became** a living soul" (Gen. 2:7). The soul of man created in chapter one was breathed into the form of man along with the Spirit of the Image of God, as the *life source* in the soul. The breath of God imparted the Seed of His Image into man and the soul of man *became* a living entity with a free will, *capable of choice*. God, who was all in one in the spirit realm—became all in one in the physical realm, in Adam.

"And the Lord God took the man, and put him into the Garden of Eden to dress and keep it. [A beautiful garden— reflecting the beautiful man—created to be God's habitation] And the Lord God commanded *the man* saying, of every tree of the garden thou mayest freely eat: but the tree of the knowledge of good and evil thou shalt not eat of it: for in the day that thou eatest thereof thou shalt surely die" (Gen. 2:15.17). "For as in Adam **all** die, even so in Christ shall **all** be made alive" (I Cor. 15:22). The definition for the word all is: the whole quantity, the *greatest extent possible*. There are *none excluded* from the all.

"And the Lord God caused a deep sleep to fall upon Adam, and he slept: and He took one of his ribs, and closed up the flesh... And the rib, which the Lord had taken from man, made He a woman and brought her to the man" (Gen. 2:21). God took DNA from Adam, in the form of a rib and created Eve. The understanding of all things created, is awaiting discovery, in both the spiritual and natural realms, such as the unfolding discoveries mapped out in our DNA, as well as things that are yet undiscovered and unseen. Removing the woman, using the man's DNA to create her as a separate entity, was because God no longer desired to be all in one—both spiritually and physically—creating two entities from one—*God was no longer all in one.*

Adam and Eve became visible forms of the invisible God, made in His Image, both male and female. "For the ***invisible*** things of Him from the creation of the world are ***clearly seen*** being ***understood by the things that are made,*** *even* ***His eternal power and Godhead***" (Rom. 1:20). Since we understand that the worlds were framed by the Word of God, so that the ***things we see*** *are* ***made of things we cannot see***—it solidifies the fact that: the invisible things of creation are the pattern in heaven for all things visible on earth. Heaven and earth—reflecting the unseen by the seen—God being the invisible, while man is the visible. God's original and ultimate plan is to become visible *in* man, uniting heaven and earth as one. "For ye are the temple of the Living God; as God hath said, ***I will dwell*** <u>***in***</u> ***them, and walk*** <u>***in***</u> *them*: and I will be their God and they shall be my people" (II Cor. 6:16).

The Fatal Choice

Before God could fully inhabit the beings He created for that purpose, they had to choose whom they would serve. Adam and Eve contained a Holy Seed, the very Image of God. When they partook of the fruit from the forbidden tree, they received another seed; a seed of willfulness and disobedience; a false image produced by a self-serving seed, contrary to the nature and character of God. They exchanged truth and life for deception and death—a very **un**profitable exchange for us *all*.

Desiring wisdom apart from God—they separated themselves—and us—from God; by believing a lie *their original identity*—became *the Lamb slain from the foundation of the world*. Choosing to disobey God's command, they brought death into their beings through the tree of the knowledge of good and evil, rather than choosing the life contained in the Tree of Life. There were only two choices: to obey God and continue *as living souls* or choose to submit to a baser nature and become lost souls in a dying body—in need of redemption.

Corruption entered into the bodies of mankind through disobedience. If not for *their act* of disobedience, the bodies formed in Genesis chapter two would have been the incorruptible dwelling place for the Spirit of God both *male* and *female*. *Disobedience robbed the entire human race in the beginning of creation*, and has been continually duplicating the same age after age, even though the consequences then and now have proven to be catastrophic.

The conditions in our world today are still reflecting the consequences brought about by one disobedient act; when Eve—then Adam entertained a suggestion—a seed in thought form, to be planted in the field of their minds. They allowed the seed to come to fruition when they partnered with it through their actions; they were changed into another image that began as a suggestion—when they were baited and beguiled with the thought: "Hath God said?" (Gen. 3:1).

God's spoken creation was altered by them through their thought creation, we are still creating ourselves and the world around us, by our thoughts and imaginings, and what they produce. That is why we are instructed to think on these things: "Finally, brethren whatsoever things are true, whatsoever things *are* honest, whatsoever things *are* just, whatsoever things *are* pure, whatsoever things *are* lovely, whatsoever things *are* of good report; if *there be* any virtue, and if *there be* any praise, think on these things" (Phil. 4:8).

Through various forms of increased communications, we are seeing and hearing the opposite of what this verse in Philippians is instructing. We are constantly being inundated with bad news traveling fast; and as appalled as we are at some of the deeds done on earth—we continue to use our purchasing power on literature and visual portrayals of these very deeds as acceptable forms of entertainment. Man has *yet* to fully comprehend, how the cause and effect of the things around him *produce* his environment.

As disobedience and the *rebellion against our own souls*, increases in intensity, so will the turmoil in the world continue to reflect it. "Know ye not, that to whom ye yield yourselves as servants to obey, his servants ye are to whom ye obey; whether of sin unto death or of obedience unto righteousness?" (Rom. 6:16). Is it possible that *even* the violent weather patterns we have been seeing recently are a reflection of an increase in violence being portrayed on earth in reality, and through means created in the imaginations of man to be conveyed as sources of entertainment? To what extent, is man the creator of his own environment? "What is man, that thou art mindful of him? Thou madest him to have dominion over the works of thy hands; thou hast put *all things* under his feet" (Ps. 8:4.6). This is a description of what God has done for man—everything else is man's creation, birthed by his thoughts and imaginings, and the results they have produced.

God communicates with us through our thoughts—*when* our receiver is properly tuned in to hear the transmission of *His still small voice*. All of the problems we face in the world today are created by the invasion of our thoughts, because first Eve and then Adam, *allowed* entrance into their thought life by entertaining a suggestion *presented to them by a deceiver*. The *de*ceiver's mission is to create static and interference, to create confusion—comparable to two stations trying to come through on one channel at the same time—to rob us of our *stability*, and prevent our *re*ceiver from hearing God, because: "A double minded man is *unstable* in *all* his ways" (James 1:8). Putting their energy in motion, by submitting themselves to another, cost them their dominion. Man retained his God given gift of choice even after he chose to share his dominion with an entity of evil intent that opposes God and man, bringing all mankind under judgment. God was chosen against and rejected, after giving man dominion over His creation—when the man chose to submit himself and his God given dominion to another—leaving God out of the equation.

We reap what we sow: the entire universe, the planets, the sun, moon and stars; are all moving in harmony with God's plan and purpose for them. Only man with his freewill and choice has rebelled against God. "For they have sown the wind, and they shall reap the whirlwind" (Hos. 8:7). God's desire is for man to be in harmony with all of His creation; then and only then, will God's will be done in earth as it is in heaven. We, who were formed from the earth, are individually and collectively, the earth that His will is to be done in.

God created, and when He finished His work *He rested*—He is still resting and beckoning us to enter into His rest. "And God did *rest* the seventh day from *all His works.* There remaineth therefore a rest to the people of God. For he that is entered into His rest, he also hath ceased from his own works as God *did* from His" (Heb. 4:4.9.10). "For thus saith the Lord God, the Holy One of Israel; in returning and rest *shall ye be saved,* in quietness and confidence shall be your strength: and ye would not" (Is. 30:15). We need to uncover and recognize the enemy of our soul—whose agenda is to keep us from hearing God and entering into His rest. It is imperative that we recognize our enemy—who he is—where he hides and how he deceives man through <u>de</u>ception blocking our <u>re</u>ception of the truth.

In the beginning, the earth was a reflection of the heavens, and the heavens were a mirror image of what existed on earth. A perfect man and perfect woman—in perfect surroundings. Disobedience on earth brought about a cataclysmic change when they were cast out of the Garden of Eden, with no access to the Tree of Life—into a place on earth that reflected the change by producing thorns and thistles, signifying the inward change in Adam and Eve. No longer were they a reflection of the garden of God's creation *within* or without. They had introduced another lineage that brought enmity against them and all of their descendants.

Standing in an ancient garden,
I was once creation's smile;
Unacquainted with deception
I was baited and beguiled.

As I cost you Lord, your children,
When the man, I did defile.
And we learned in desolation,
To know death—complete and vile.

Now I bring a precious ointment,
In an alabaster box.
Only you, Beloved Savior,
Truly comprehend the cost.

I bring to you the essence
And the substance of my soul,
And I pour it out upon you
Who always could behold:

Your child within the woman
And the heart within the child,
Longing to stand in Eden,
Un-afraid, and un-beguiled.

We see the manifestation of consequences emerging, when Cain, being a man of the field—representing the seed of man—slew his brother Abel, a shepherd, who represented the Seed of the Image of God. Consequences that were the result of the *chosen* disobedience of Adam and Eve were portrayed in a visible act when Cain killed Abel; reflecting on earth what was first done in the invisible realm of the Spirit, when Adam and Eve *chose* to exercise their God given—gift of free will—against God's will.

An invisible thought always precedes a visible act; that is why our thoughts and imaginings need to be brought into subjection and held in check, instead of being allowed to run rampant through our minds of their own volition. We need to guard our thoughts, because like seeds, they produce actions when we nurture them and give them ground to be imbedded in us. Each thought is a living entity that is capable of producing emotion. **E-motion** is energy in motion—giving our thoughts the power to either redeem or enslave us. Thoughts like seeds produce after their own kind: our idle thoughts are no longer idle when they become partnered with and activated by our emotions.

Cain's jealousy and resentment toward his brother began as a seed in his thoughts—as he continued to nurture ill will toward Abel, his jealousy produced anger that erupted into an emotional act of violence. An act of violence—set in motion by their parents before Cain and Abel were born—a visible portrayal of the enmity produced on earth through the disobedience of their parents.

The Blood of Abel

"By faith Abel offered unto God a more excellent sacrifice than Cain, by which he obtained witness that he was righteous, God testifying of his gifts: and by it he being dead *yet* speaketh" (Heb. 11:4) "Not as Cain, who was of that wicked one, and slew his brother. And wherefore slew he him? Because his own works were evil, and his brothers righteous" (I John 3:12).

Their offerings identified them and represented *who they were*. "Cain brought of the fruit of the ground an offering unto the Lord. And Abel, he also brought of the firstlings of his flock and the fat thereof. And the Lord had respect unto Abel, and to his offering:

But unto Cain he had not respect. And Cain was very wroth, [angry] and his countenance fell" (Gen. 4:4.5). Looking at this from the viewpoint of the natural man, may incur sympathy for Cain's plight, but his offering was one from the natural man he represented, the fallen nature that cannot please God—a strange vine not of His planting. Abel, however, being the express Image of God, who himself was to become **an unwilling victim** as **a Lamb slain for the deeds of his parents**, offered unto God the firstlings of his flock, a sacrificial blood offering. Abel, *becoming a sacrificial lamb,* was subsequent to *his offering* of a *sacrificial* lamb from the firstlings of his flock.

"And it came to pass, when they were in the field, that Cain rose up against Abel his brother, and slew him. And the Lord said unto Cain where *is* Abel thy brother? And he said, I know not: *Am* I my brother's keeper? And He said what hast thou done? **The voice of thy brother's blood, crieth** unto me from the ground" (Gen. 4:8-10). *"He being dead yet speaketh"* (Heb. 11:4).

"The Lamb slain from the foundation of the world" (Rev. 13:8). The blood of Abel, being the visible portrayal of that slain Lamb, crying to God from the ground—was the result of the slaying of the Lamb by the entrance of death into existence *within* Adam and Eve—foreshadowing the coming of Jesus as the Lamb slain to take away sin once and for all. It is extremely important that we realize that the blood of Abel crying out to God from the ground, is a visible portrayal of an *inward reality* in the invisible realm of the spirit. The Lamb slain from the foundation of the world affects us all. Every one born on the earth in an *earthen vessel* is replicating Adam and Eve's sin of shedding the blood of the Lamb *within them*. We have *within us* the blood stain of the slain Lamb *crying out* from *our* ground.

Redemption through the blood of Jesus is *absolutely necessary*, to cleanse us from *all stain* of original sin. Man has carried the *blood stain* of the Lamb since the foundation of the world from generation to generation, until Jesus came and washed it away with His own *sinless* blood. **Abel's blood** was **unwillingly shed**—because sin entered into the world—**Jesus's blood** was **willing shed** to take away sin, as the ultimate sacrifice for sin, cancelling the debt once and *for all*. His blood cleansed us from sin—however, blood stains always leave an imprint that can be detected. To *receive* the depth of cleansing to remove *all stain of original sin imprinted* within us, we are blessed with retaining the God given gift of our *power of choice* that en*ables* us to choose to receive the redemption provided for us through the cleansing power of the blood of Jesus Christ.

"And Adam knew his wife again; and she bare a son and called his name Seth: For God, *said she*, hath *appointed* me **another seed** [Seed of God] instead of Abel, whom Cain slew" (Gen. 4:25). "And Adam lived an hundred and thirty years, and **begat** a son **in his own likeness, after his image**: and called his name Seth" (Gen. 5:3).

In Adam and Eve the two seeds—two identities were both present when Seth was conceived—producing after their own image and likeness: Seth contained in *one body* both seeds—the Immortal Seed of God and the mortal seed of the natural man.

Summary: We have been made aware of our origin, and how we came into the complexity of our being. We will now see how God is going to produce His **remarkable** plan through the dilemma man's disobedience has gotten him into; as He **re-marks-Abel,** through Jesus Christ. The Spirit of God is not complicated: "Hear, O Israel: **the Lord our God is one** Lord" (Deut. 6:4). God is **one Lord**–He was **all in one**—*desiring to be all in all.* Man *complicates the simplicity of God,* keeping the soul in a state of confusion and unrest. Man's duality of good and evil keeps him in constant confusion and turmoil as he tries to juggle the fruit from the forbidden tree in his effort to understand the complexity of his being. There is no unity in the tree of the knowledge of good and evil, it is a house divided that cannot stand and does not contain—nor can it ever yield *life* producing fruit, its foundation—based on a lie from the beginning, produces conflict and its fruit is death. May the Holy Spirit, *hasten* to unravel the tapestry, being woven with threads from the tree of the knowledge of good and evil—by a seed that in secret—plots and schemes against mankind. There is no duality or conflict in the Tree of Life. The foundation of the Tree of Life is rooted and grounded in the Truth, and its fruit is Life. Our souls, like snowflakes, differ one from another, no two being exactly alike. Our unique individuality is revealed in the nature of our soul. God's original plan—was and still is, to be our true source of energy in motion, the intended life source in the soul—as we partake of the Tree of Life whose Seed is in the midst of the garden *in* our soul.

Chapter Two

Reclaimed Through Obedience

What was lost through disobedience; must be reclaimed through obedience. The *reversal* of the previous order of things—occurring first in the spirit realm—then reflected on earth can be clearly seen; now before God will accomplish His wonders among us, He must *first find faith* on earth. The Old Testament is a treasure trove of references to God making covenants with chosen men and women to reveal faith, through their obedience. God was working in unison with them by securing agreements through their obedience to unfold His redemptive plan to bring us back to His original purpose for man.

It was His Seed in man to whom He gave dominion over the earth before the soul, being capable of choice, allowed the entrance of an enemy seed to usurp his God given dominion, by allowing deception to produce disobedience in him. The seed that produced the natural man appointed to death—entered Eve, then Adam in the form of a *thought* that produced doubt—resulting in unbelief when they questioned God's intentions.

"And it came to pass, when men [seed of Cain] began to multiply on the earth and daughters were born unto them, That the sons of God [children of Seth—the lineage containing God's Seed] saw the daughters of men that they *were* fair and they took them wives of all which they chose. And the Lord said, my Spirit will not always strive with man... they bare *children* to them, the same *became* mighty men which were of old, men of renown. And God saw that wickedness of man *was* great in the earth, and *that **every imagination** of the **thoughts*** of his heart *was* only evil continually" (Gen. 6:1-5). They were *incapable* of contributing anything of value to God's creation. God forbid that we who now inhabit the earth would ever digress and degrade to that extreme.

God sent a flood to destroy all that had been produced by the Seed of Seth co-mingling with the seed of Cain, so the race of mankind could continue through a remnant of the chosen lineage of Seth, through Noah and his sons, who contained both the Seed of God and the seed of *man's own creation*. God's purpose in sending the flood was to destroy those who contained an extra portion—a double portion of Cain. God repented that He had made man, because the earth was corrupt and filled with violence. The Holy Seed, through Seth's sons co-mingling with the seed of evildoers through Cain's daughters, created a lineage that was intolerable with God.

God's Covenant with Noah

Noah, a descendant of Seth, was the only descendant remaining in that lineage, who found grace in the eyes of the Lord, and walked with God, obeying Him by building an ark: an act of faith necessary to produce a new beginning for mankind. Through his act of obedience Noah was able to save a portion of what God created while God cleansed the land of all that offended Him. "But Noah found grace in the eyes of the Lord… Noah was a just man *and* perfect in his generations, *and* Noah walked with God" (Gen. 6:8.9). It was through Noah's obedience in building an ark that he and his whole family were saved from the destruction that came upon the earth. "And I will establish my *covenant* with you; neither shall all flesh be cut off any more by the water of a flood; neither shall there anymore be a flood to destroy the earth" (Gen. 9:11). "But as the days of Noah were so shall the coming of the Son of Man be" (Matt. 24:37).

Noah, a descendant of Seth, found grace in the eyes of the Lord, as a chosen vessel containing the Seed of the Image of God. "..Noah only, remained alive, and they that were with him in the ark" (Gen. 7:23). All else was destroyed by the flood, so will it be when Jesus returns—all that is not covered under the blood covenant of grace and does not reflect His Image will be destroyed by the fire of His presence. If not for the covenant God made with Noah, the earth as we know it would probably not be in existence. The earth as it is today would certainly be in for another dip. "…for the imagination of man's heart is evil from his youth: neither will I again smite anymore everything living, as I have done. While the earth remaineth seedtime and harvest, and cold and heat, and summer and winter…day and night shall not cease" (Gen. 8:21).

Jesus came from the bosom of His Father to herald a new creation just as the dove flew from the bosom of Noah to herald the beginning of a new world, reborn—cleansed of unrighteousness. The earth was cleansed by a baptism of water through the flood, and then resurrected—producing new life—comparable to Jesus's baptism—representing His death, burial and resurrection—producing new life for man.

Noah had three sons, Shem, Japheth and Ham. Noah was lying drunk and uncovered in his tent from sampling to much of the wine from his vineyard.

"And *Ham* the father of *Canaan,* saw the nakedness of his father, and told his two brethren…And Shem and Japheth took a garment and laid it upon their shoulders and went backwards and covered the nakedness of their father… And Noah awoke from his wine, and knew what his younger son had done unto him. And he said cursed be Canaan; a servant of servants shall he be unto his brethren. And he said, blessed be the Lord God of Shem; and Canaan shall be his servant. God shall enlarge Japheth and he shall dwell in the tents of Shem; and Canaan shall be his servant" (Gen. 9:23-27).

We can rightly divide the Word of God and see the natures of Noah's sons revealed through their actions. Noah blessed the God of Shem—the lineage through which the Seed of the Image of God would continue through the generations, He blessed Japheth to dwell in the tents of Shem, revealing Japheth as a *type* of the soul. Ham, who was revealed to be *a type of* the cursed one, represents the lineage of the fallen nature of the man of sin continuing through the generations of man. Noah's three sons are a type and parable of the spirit, soul and flesh of man. The nature of Ham, seen in the attempts of man, in defiance of God, to build a tower to heaven is a picture of the activity of the man of sin—creating the necessity for God—to divide the earth into many *nations* and *nationalities*.

The tower of Babel is where the Lord confused the language of the people and divided the earth into many nations and languages, a change that was necessary, to create disharmony among them—to prevent them from propagating their evil intent against God and man. "And the Lord said: Behold, the people is one, and they have all one language; and this they begin to do; and now nothing will be restrained from them, *which they have imagined to do*" (Gen. 11:6). This verifies the power contained in our thoughts and imaginings especially when there is agreement and unity among us. They had the audacity to try to build a tower to heaven—which was no threat because it was impossible to do. It was the spirit behind their deed that caused the Lord to bring confusion into their midst. "For thou has said in thine heart, I will ascend into heaven, I will exalt my throne above the stars of God…" (Is. 14:13). God's covenant with Noah prevented Him from taking more drastic measures. Thank God, His covenant with Noah has held throughout the ages or it is very possible the earth would no longer be inhabited by man.

The world is reeling to and fro with confusion: Babel and Babylon are synonymous with confusion. What is the meaning of the great mystery Babylon? Consider this: could it simply be what is indicated? Mystery, that creates confusion—mystery being a by-product of confusion and lack of understanding. Is it possible that the great harlot of confusion is *simply* the blindness cast over the face of the people to keep them from *understanding* the *truth* and the *light of life* that is found only in Christ Jesus? Where truth and understanding abide there can be no confusion. "Come now, and let us reason together saith the Lord" (Is. 1:18).

The forbidden tree in the Garden of Eden produced both good and evil, so even the good in the fallen nature of man produces death. "Babylon the great is fallen, is fallen, and is become the habitation of devils, and the hold of every foul spirit, and a cage of every unclean and hateful bird" (Rev. 18:2). *Her name is mystery*—*her nature* is to sow and nurture seeds of doubt and unbelief—*her mission* is to create confusion and blindness to keep man from the knowledge of the truth and purpose for his existence. She uses the systems and lures of this world to seduce man, to keep him distracted and in bondage to personal power, personal gain and the desires of the flesh—she thrives on the battles produced by the conflict between good and evil. The tree of the knowledge of good and evil produces death, however, we are told: "Be not overcome with evil, but overcome evil with good" (Rom. 12:21). It is better to choose the good and abhor the evil, for our own sakes and for those around us, however it is *necessary* that we: "*Seek God* [rather than good] and not evil that *ye may live*" (Amos 5:14).

The beast spoken of in connection with the mother of harlots in the book of Revelation, ***that was*** and **is *not***, and ***yet is***—speaks of the Cross where the beast was overcome and is not—but yet is—because of the blindness cast over the people that gives it power through misdirected faith. Through a lack of understanding concerning the power of the Cross we give ***power*** and ***strength,*** through confusion to what we believe to be true—though it be deception.

"These have one mind, and shall give their ***power*** and ***strength*** unto the beast. These shall make war with the Lamb and the Lamb shall overcome them: For He is Lord of lords, and King of kings: and they that are with Him *are **called*** and *chosen,* and *faithful.* [God's Seed] And He saith unto me, the waters which thou sawest, where the whore sitteth, are peoples, and multitudes, and nations, and tongues. For God hath put in their hearts to fulfill His will, and to agree, and give their kingdom unto the beast, until the Words of God shall be fulfilled. And the woman which thou sawest is that great city, which reigneth over the kings of the earth" (Rev. 17: 13-15.17.18). The natural man, who knows not his maker, utilizes his *power* and *strength* for a life without substance.

The nature of the seed in man that causes him to sin is to make war with the Lamb. Thank God, the Lamb has already overcome that unholy seed, of this there is no doubt—it was accomplished on the Cross. There remains a hindrance to the full manifestation of God in the earth, because, through deception, man shared his God given dominion with the seed that causes him to sin—only man can take it back by his power of choice through faith—submitting himself to the Spirit of Truth—which is the Holy Spirit, sent to be our Comforter—to lead us into all truth.

God's Promise to Abraham

The truest test of man's obedience came through Abraham, earning him the title: father of our faith, because he was willing to leave all that was familiar to him and go into an unfamiliar—uninhabited land. *His* act of faith in offering his only son Isaac by obeying God's command was his *ultimate* act of obedience—providing the necessary faith on earth for God to offer *His* only begotten Son. "When the Son of man cometh, shall He find faith on earth?" (Luke 18:8). Abraham is called the father of our faith, while his son Isaac is called the son of promise; because of the covenant God made with Abraham of a supernatural intervention in producing an heir through Sarah—who had long passed the age of childbearing.

The willfulness of humanity resurfaced, taking action through natural reasoning, when Sarah convinced Abraham to produce seed by her handmaiden, an Egyptian whose name was Hagar. Rather than trusting and waiting for the Lord's timing, she succeeded in duplicating Eve's action by going beyond the covenant with God, when she convinced Abraham to produce seed through Hagar—after God had made a covenant with him concerning his Seed. The fruit of their actions produced a different lineage—contrary to the one God had promised.

It is in the human nature, to attempt to fulfill what God has revealed, when only the Lord Himself can bring to pass in the fullness of time, what He has promised. Our contribution is to receive by faith—to believe and trust Him to accomplish what He has promised. The revelation declared in this book was given, July 16-24, 1971, a long gestation period of forty years—held in the womb of conception in the soul until the *fullness of time* for the revealing—there were a few unsuccessful attempts to birth it prematurely, before it became obvious it was for *an appointed time* that had not *yet* come.

"Now to Abraham and his Seed were the promises made. He saith not to seeds, as of many but as of *one* and to thy Seed which is Christ" (Gal. 3:16). God told Abraham that in Isaac his Seed would be called. This calling first occurred in Jacob, and through his lineage, in Jesus, as the Son of Man. All who were born through Noah after the flood came through the lineage of Seth. He was born to Adam and Eve in their likeness, containing both The Seed of God and a seed that opposes God, as well as opposing the soul of man created in the Image of God.

The importance of the woman's role cannot be diminished— Abraham produced other seed but it took a Sarah to produce an Isaac; it was *chosen women,* as well as chosen men—who produced *the chosen Seed.* The Old Testament record containing testimony of how God chose certain women to produce the promised Seed is clearly seen in the New Testament account of Mary—a virgin, bringing forth the ultimate Seed of Promise—a uniquely, supernatural occurrence of which all that preceded it were types and shadows of barren women unable to conceive by natural means.

"Isaac entreated the Lord for his wife, because she was barren: and the Lord was entreated of him, and Rebekah his wife conceived… And the children struggled together within her; and she said, *if it be so* why *am* I thus? And the Lord said unto her, Two nations *are* in thy womb, and two manner of people shall be separated out of thy bowels; and the *one people* shall be stronger than the *other people*; and the elder shall serve the younger.

"And when her days to be delivered were fulfilled, behold, there were twins in her womb, the first came out red, [earthy] all over like an hairy garment, and they called his name Esau [Esau, the elder represented the express image of the natural man]. "And after that came his brother out, and his hand took hold on Esau's heel; and his name was called Jacob" [Jacob, the younger represented the express Image of the Seed of God] (Gen. 25:21-23.25.26).

"Now this was *the manner* in former time in Israel concerning **redeeming** and concerning **changing,** for to confirm all things;

*a man **plucked off his shoe**, and gave *it* to his neighbor; and this *was* a testimony in Israel" (Ruth 4:7). In taking hold on Esau's heel, Jacob was establishing his claim on the birthright from the womb. This incident between Jacob and Esau could very well be where the custom concerning **redeeming** and **changing** began. It could also be the meaning behind John the Baptist's words describing Jesus. "He it is, who coming after me, is preferred before me, **whose shoe's latchet** *I am not worthy* **to unloose.** [His recognition of Jesus as the Lamb of God; caused him to feel unworthy to baptize Jesus, the **redeemer,** who came to **change** the world] "This is He of whom I said, "After me cometh a man which is preferred before me: for He was before me" (John 1:27.30).

Innocence Contested

We come forth from our mother's womb with the seed of two nations within us: it could also be said to be two kingdoms, or two natures within us. Our innocence as children is not fully contested until we reach the age of puberty, when physically the changes that occur are hormonal—a time of vulnerability and confusion—during the transition period between childhood and becoming an adult. Spiritually, it is when we are the most vulnerable, that our natural man—*represented in type* as the nation of Esau, rises up to struggle with our souls to increase his dominion over us and challenge our innocence—to conceal and try to abort our true identity, by attempting to super-impose a false one in its place.

The method has always been the same—making us feel like we are somehow inferior, so the real us hides for fear of failure to measure up in the eyes of others, which causes us to accept a false persona of *confusing* and *conflicting* things, instead of becoming who we really are intended to be—a vessel created to express the Image of a Holy God.

> Pieces and patches make nothing sublime
> Burlap and satin—some shadow some shine.
> Christ here—me there; some false and some fine.
> Give me a pull—I'll unwind.
>
> Partly I'm winter and partly I'm spring,
> Mostly confusion—conflicting things,
> Call for the lilies—weeds will I bring'
> Only my Lord hears me sing.

The rebellion that sometimes accompanies the teenage years—occurs when the nation of Esau (*natural man*) rises up to struggle with our souls for dominion, creating *confusion* and *conflict*. Our main line of defense is to yield ourselves to the same *power* that gave Jacob victory over Esau, the power of God. Redemption—activated in our lives through Jesus Christ—puts us in a place of greater advantage by giving us *power* for victory through the Holy Spirit.

It is a time of choosing whom we will serve, the Image of God or the image of man. Jesus came in the flesh, representing both the Seed of God and the seed of man, to break every yoke, and undo our heavy burdens and let our oppressed souls go free. We have—and we hold, the *choice* to determine how much ground is retained by our true identity, and how much is forfeited to the formation of a false image, being produced through the enticements of the world around us and the genetics of the natural man. Adam and Eve *hid* from God in the garden, after sin entered into them. Man's soul has an innate tendency to *hide*, giving more ground to the false image produced through the natural man.

"And the boys grew; Esau was a *cunning* hunter, a man of the field; [as Cain before him] And Jacob *was* a *plain* man, dwelling in tents" (Gen. 25:27). The Ark of the Covenant, like Jacob, was housed in a tent. The two seeds born separate in Cain and Abel were the result of Adam and Eve bearing fruit after their own kind: in the likeness of the heavenly design— Abel, and in the likeness of their own design through their disobedience—Cain. Their choice created a dual rather than a singular identity. The two seeds entered them separately; revealing the two separate identities through Cain and Abel. Cain—being of that wicked one and Abel—the Seed of the righteousness of God.

Summary: Disobedience separated man from God in an instant, and it has taken a long and winding road through the centuries to bring us back. What began at creation as a perfect reflection of heaven on earth—was distorted through deception that produced disobedience. The long and winding road through the wilderness of man's own creation—became an earth that was no longer a reflection of heaven. Through His Word, God has given us a map to follow, that leads us through the birth, crucifixion, and resurrection of Jesus Christ. Jesus, coming to earth as a reflection of heaven on earth—became the key to unwinding the path of desolation carved into the souls of mankind. Through His obedience He reconciled us to God. Adam was *created*, and then *formed*; Jesus was the only begotten, and we who were formed in our mother's womb, are being transformed by the renewing of our minds, as His Word is written in our hearts. The angel of the Lord rolling away the stone from Jesus's tomb, was a parable—of an agreement on earth in the spirit realm for Jesus to roll the stony heart of duality away from our soul and release the new creation life from the place of its en**tomb**ment within us. "And I will give them one heart, and I will put a new Spirit within you; and I will take the stony heart out of their flesh, and will give them a heart of flesh" (Ez. 11:19). It is an exchanged life—from an error encrusted hardened heart—to the Spirit of Truth, Mercy and Love in a tender heart—*a very profitable exchange for us all.*

Chapter Three

Jacob's True Identity Revealed

The Separation

The two seeds, combined in Seth, were once again *separated* from Rebekah's womb in Esau and Jacob, so that Jacob, whose name means *supplanter,* could *fulfill his destiny* by supplanting Esau. Getting the birthright and blessing was his mission, and it was necessary that he fulfill his mission in order to prepare the way for the coming of our salvation.

"And Isaac loved Esau because he did eat of his venison: but Rebekah loved Jacob" (Gen. 25:28). Isaac was **called** the son of promise, Jacob was the fulfillment of the promise God made to Abraham. "In Isaac shall thy Seed be **called**" (Rom. 9:6). Jacob was the seed spoken of; he being the *chosen* Seed separated out and **called** forth from Rebekah's womb. Abraham received a blessing with promise for his Seed; Isaac was the conduit for the Seed to be passed on and *separated from Rebekah's womb,* to be **called** *forth in Jacob*—through His lineage: the tribe of Judah—*Jesus was* **called** *forth, from* *the womb of the Virgin Mary.* Shedding His blood on the Cross for our redemption enabled Jesus to be the conduit for the Holy Spirit to be passed on to dwell in us to complete God's plan for His Seed in man to be **called** forth—to be birthed from the womb of our soul.

Esau came from the field faint with hunger, since he was a man driven by his appetites, he did not value his birthright above having his hunger satisfied; when Jacob offered him food in exchange for his birthright, his reply was: "Behold I *am* at the point to die: and what profit shall this birthright do me?" (Gen. 25:32). Esau had no vision beyond having his physical needs met.

When realizing we lack the strength to make it on our own and we call out to God, His ear is ever open to hear the cry of our *soul*. "He shall call upon me, and I will answer him: *I will be* with him in trouble; I will deliver him, and honor him" (Ps. 91:15). When in trouble and our *souls* cry out to the Lord, *exercising our power of choice*; we trade our natural birthright for our spiritual heritage as children of the Living God through the true supplanter—Jesus Christ. He supplants our old nature with our true birthright that was usurped through deception in the beginning. Jacob was retrieving the birthright from the natural man that rightfully belonged to him—and to every soul through God's Seed in **all** mankind, according to the covenant God made with Abraham: "In Isaac shall thy Seed be *called*" (Gen.21:12).

The third chapter of Galatians says of Abraham: "Abraham believed God and it was accounted to him for righteousness… They which are of faith, [God's Seed] the same are the children of Abraham… In thee shall **all nations** be blessed. Christ hath redeemed us from the curse of the law, being made a curse for us: for it is written, Cursed *is* every one that hangeth on a tree: That the blessing of Abraham might come on the Gentiles through Jesus Christ" (Gal. 3:6-8.13). What began *with* a tree was ended *on* a tree. The tree of the knowledge of good and evil crucified the Lamb *in* Adam and Eve at the foundation of the world. Jesus willing permitted himself to be nailed to a cross, made from a tree, cancelling out the original murder of the Lamb—*visibly* portrayed when Cain killed Abel. Offering His life as an atonement—**Christ redeemed us all**—none are excluded—the all includes all nationalities—every nation kindred and tongue.

Isaac being the chosen Seed did not exclude Abraham's other children from being his seed. After Sarah's death he took another wife, Ketura—who produced seven additional sons with Abraham. Sarah was a chosen woman—as were Rebekah, Rachel, and Mary the mother of Jesus, among others. Hannah was the favored wife, loved by her husband, "… but the Lord had shut her womb. And her adversary [Peninnah] provoked her sore, for to make her fret, because the Lord had shut her womb" (I Sam. 1:5-6).

> "Oh Hannah!" calls Peninnah,
> "Where are your sons?"
> Look I have ten children;
> You don't have one!"
>
> "Oh Hannah!" Mocks Peninnah,
> "Our husband favors you,
> But you can't give him children,
> What good does it do?"

"Dear Hannah," soothed the Father,
Hannah, you are mine.
Trust me and remember,
Samuels take time."

There are none excluded from containing the Seed of God. Jacob—Israel had twelve sons, Joseph receiving the double portion—a greater blessing, did not exclude the other eleven from being the children of Israel. God spoke to Abraham saying: "And I will make thy seed as the dust of the earth: so that *if* a man can number the dust of the earth, *then* shall thy seed also be numbered" (Gen. 13:16). We who were formed from the dust of the earth have the Seed of God lying dormant in our earthen vessels, until it is *revived* through faith in Jesus Christ, who came as the express Image of that Seed. It is faith that calls the Seed out of retirement into *renewed activity*—as portrayed in type through Abraham and Sarah—in producing the son of promise. The deadness of Sarah's womb, being *renewed* to produce the son of promise—is a parable of the deadness within our soul, being *renewed,* by the *transfusion of life* though the blood of Jesus, enabling us to be born again—*renewing life* to the dormant Seed of the Image of God within us.

Isaac was the son of promise because he was the lineage through which Jesus Christ—God's only begotten Son of promise, as the Son of Man would be called "the son of David, the son of Abraham" (Matt. 1:1). It is in the competitive nature of the natural man to compare one against another. No one has to consider it a loss for someone to win. We need to comprehend that *we have all won* and become *one* through the victory of Jesus Christ—the Seed of God—our true heritage.

We become willing to relinquish our natural birthright to God, through Jesus Christ when we realize that we no longer have the ability to effectively continue on our self-reliant path. *When our soul **repents** for submitting to the man of sin, that works through the natural man, and we turn from our feeble attempt of existing in what we heretofore thought was our identity*—we are changed from death to life. We are *all* potentially children of God, some are alive with life—others remain dormant, or somewhere in the twilight zone, until our souls are fully awakened. "Awake, awake, put on strength, O arm of the Lord; awake, as in the **generations of old**" [before Adam and Eve chose to serve another] (Is. 51:9). The Seed of God remains dormant, until *our souls are awakened* to the truth of the reality of the presence of God within us.

"The children which thou shalt have, after thou hast lost the other, shall say again in thine ears, The place *is* too straight for me: give place to me that I may dwell, Then shalt thou say in thine heart, Who hath begotten me these, seeing I have lost my children, and am desolate, *a captive and removing to and fro?* And who hath brought up these? Behold, I was left alone; these, where *had* they *been?* (Is. 49:20.21). This scripture is describing the children we have lost, as being the part of us produced through the souls union with the natural man—a false identity—leaving us *desolate* with the awareness that all we have produced is without substance and cannot sustain us.

When we are awakened to the awareness of our desolation and receive the benefits of the Cross, our eyes are opened to see *a part of us* that we were not aware of existing. The children we have after we are no longer serving the man of sin through the natural man—is our true identity—God's original design for us produced through our soul in union with the Seed of God—a *new* creation, that in reality is the *original creation*, although it's presence within us *seems* new to us. "Enlarge the place of thy tent, and let them stretch forth the curtains of thine habitations: spare not lengthen the cords, and strengthen thy stakes for thou shalt break forth on the right hand and on the left…" (Is. 54: 2-3). The Seed of the Image of God, since the beginning of time, waiting patiently to be acknowledged—is saying in our ears, move over give me some space so that I can live the life through you that we were intended to live. "Where had these been?" They were there all the time, *waiting*, until we become *desolate* enough to see that we are beyond our natural ability to sustain ourselves apart from divine intervention; an intervention that *must be requested*—by invitation, through an agreement from the *choice* of our souls—before intervening.

The Immaculate Conception

Through an Immaculate Conception, we are born anew by the working of the Holy Spirit. The term: born again, denotes a rebirth of what previously existed. It is then our true identity, as the Seed of the Image of God, which has remained dormant since it was slain at the beginning of creation, is reborn and resurrected in us. Jesus, born of a virgin, through an Immaculate Conception by the Holy Spirit, made it possible for us to be born again through the same process of being conceived immaculately, to walk in newness of life. He came as the Seed of God matured to its full potential to reveal our true identity containing the *same* Seed—with the *same* potential for maturity—activated by *the same* Holy Spirit.

"And the Angel answered and said unto her, "The Holy Ghost shall come upon thee, and the power of the Highest shall overshadow thee; therefore, also that Holy thing which shall be born of thee shall be called the Son of God" (Luke.1:35). In like manner, *at our invitation* the Holy Ghost comes upon us and overshadows us—*renewing life* to the Seed that was man's true identity at creation. Jesus's birth in a stable was no happenstance—it perfectly depicts the conditions He finds Himself in when His Seed is reborn in us. He came to us, born in a lowly stable, putting Himself on our level to bring us up to His.

The Lord has drawn us a picture,
A silent majestic view,
Christ comes forth in a stable,
When He's born in me and you.

May our hearts become like Mary's,
And yield to the Holy Birth.
While our souls like His Blessed Mother,
Travail as He's born in our earth.

The portrayal is God's repetition:
The coming of Christ to earth.
And His presence in us increases,
Our simple Habitat's worth.

As He draws us on to His level,
He changes our lowly estate,
And we become more than a stable,
As trusting in His love we wait.

Jesus didn't come to exalt Himself, or to be exalted. He came as the visible image of who we really are, who we were created to be at the beginning of creation, when we were created in the Image of God. Adam and Eve, having dominion, possessing a free will to choose—*recreated themselves* into another image by their choice to be independent of God. Through Jesus Christ and His sacrifice and the redemption through His blood we can *choose to be transformed* into His Image. "Because as He is so are we in this world" (I John 4:1.7).

"In Isaac shall thy Seed be **called**. They which are the **children of the flesh**, [seed of the natural man] these **are not the children of God**; but the children of the promise are counted for the Seed" [God's Seed of promise is *hidden* in every one of us] (Rom. 9:8).

A Single Lump of Clay

"When Rebekah had conceived by one, *even* our father Isaac, for *the children* being not yet born, neither having done any good or evil, that the purpose of God according to election might stand, not of works, but of him that **calleth**; it was said unto her, The elder shall serve the younger. As it is written, Jacob have I loved, but Esau I have hated. What shall we say then? *Is there* unrighteousness with God? God forbid. Nay O man, who art thou that repliest against God shall the thing *formed* say to Him that *formed* it, why has thou *made me thus*?" (Rom. 9:10-14.20). This portion of scripture clearly states that **We who were formed from the dust of the earth** are made thus: each one of us, containing in our form one that God loves and one that God hates, it also reveals that God knew there would be a reaction to His saying He hated Esau; to understand His statement calls for rightly dividing the Word of God.

The truth of the matter can be clearly seen, by rightly dividing the Word of God, whose sword of the Spirit, rightly divides man, not from others, but from himself, within himself. Both seeds were housed in Rebekah's womb, just as they are both housed in our lump of clay. She was told that two nations were in her womb—the two nations, were two natures—just as within each of us, we have the nature of the natural man we are born with, and the nature of God lying dormant in Seed form, ready to be activated when we *choose* to be born again by the Immaculate Conception of the Holy Spirit.

"Hath not the potter power over the clay, of the ***same lump*** [one body] to make one vessel unto honor [Seed of God] another unto dishonor? [seed of disobedience] And that He might make known the riches of His glory on the ***vessels of mercy,*** which He had afore prepared unto glory" (Rom. 9:21-23).

The ***same lump*** is the singular lump of clay from which man was formed, containing one Seed—the Seed of God, ***a vessel of honor.*** A suggestion was presented to Adam and Eve, and by acting on it they partook of another seed that created in them ***a vessel of dishonor***—thus the *two seeds* were housed in the ***same lump.***

"For whom He did foreknow, [His Seed] He also did predestinate *to be* conformed to the Image of His Son, that He might be the *firstborn among many* brethren. Moreover, whom He did predestinate, them He also called: and whom He ***called,*** them He also justified: and whom He justified them He also glorified" (Rom. 8:29.30). There is a doctrine of predestination—believed by some, that is the result of misinterpreting this passage of scripture in Paul's letter to the Romans, claiming that one individual is predestined to glory and another to dishonor. Thank God when the Word is rightly divided, this is clearly not the truth. Paul is a prime example of one whose deeds, performed according to the nature of his natural man—would have categorized him as a vessel of dishonor. If God had not made provision for the salvation of *all mankind* through Jesus Christ, there would have been no hope or mercy for Saul, who became the new creation Paul—an immediate revelation of what Jesus died for, is seen through Saul's awesome conversion through a rebirth, to become Paul the apostle of Jesus Christ.

The *erroneous doctrine* derived from the misinterpretation of scripture concerning predestination, leaves some without hope of salvation, when Paul clearly states that the same lump of clay from which man was formed, contains both honor and dishonor, a fact that he became well aware of from his own conversion experience. Many have been discouraged to the point of despair over this *doctrine of error,* especially when the accuser of the brethren, the enemy of their soul plants the thought in their minds that they are among those destined to be lost. Sadly, there are those who have been exposed to this teaching, who truly believe this deception, and have no hope, because of their belief that they are among those *destined* to be lost.

Another deception used to torment and take away hope, is when a soul is deceived into thinking they have committed the unpardonable sin. *Sin was terminated on the Cross.* He who is born of God does not sin, speaks of the Seed of God, the true identity of our soul. The false identity that serves the man of sin is the one that is unpardonable—its foundation based on a lie from the beginning. The tares-parasites and the chaff on our souls, will be shaken loose and consumed by fire. "Whose fan *is* in His hand, and *He will thoroughly purge His floor,* and *gather His* wheat *into the garner*; but He will burn up the chaff with unquenchable fire" (Matt. 3:12). It is important that we realize that *we are His wheat*—we are *not* the chaff. The wheat *is gathered* into His barn, not burned. A more detailed description of the parallel between the wheat and the soul can be found in chapter five.

We can all identify with Paul's—Romans chapter seven syndrome—where he describes the two warring factions in himself. "For the good that I would, I do not, but evil which I would not, that I do. Now if I do that I would not, it is no more I that do it, but sin [dishonor] that dwelleth in me... bringing me into captivity to the law of sin which is in my members. O wretched man that I am! Who shall deliver me from the body of this death?" (Rom. 7:19.20.23.24). Jesus died for the ungodly, for all have sinned, and are in need of redemption through His blood, to *revive* the Seed of God's original creation within us, that remains dormant until it is *regenerated* by the Holy Spirit.

John the Baptist said: "Ye yourselves bear me witness that I said I am not the Christ, but that I am sent before him. He must increase, but I must decrease" (John 3:28.30). Through the power of the Holy Spirit at work in us, the natural man must decrease so that God's Seed within us can increase, *through* **repentance** *and the renewing of our minds*—receiving the mind of Christ. "Till *we* **all** come in the unity of the faith, and of the knowledge of the Son of God unto a **perfect** *man,* unto the *measure* of the stature of the **fullness** of Christ; That we *henceforth* be no more children, tossed to and fro and carried about with every wind of doctrine, by the sleight of men, and cunning craftiness, whereby they lie in wait to deceive; [seed in the natural man] But speaking the truth in love, may grow up *into Him* in all things, which is the **head** *even* Christ" (Eph. 4:13-15).

"Also I heard the voice of the Lord, saying, Whom shall I send, and who will go for **us**? Then said I, *here I am; send me.* And He said Go, and tell this people, Hear ye indeed, but understand not; and see ye indeed, but perceive not. [natural man] Make the heart of this people fat, and make their ears heavy, and shut their eyes, lest they see with their eyes and hear with their ears, and understand with their heart, and convert, and be healed" (Is. 6:8-10).

The Seed of God in man can both *hear* and *see*—the Word when heard, leaves the natural man desolate without understanding to convert and be healed, because it is foolishness to him. The Word brings life to our soul so we can convert and be healed—by making the right *choice* as to whom we will serve—when we are brought to a place of *repentance* by recognizing the desolation in our lives that is produced by the man of sin working through the natural man.

As a small acorn contains the full potential of producing a giant tree—the Seed of God contains the complete nature, character and Image of God, ready to be reproduced, in us as from glory to glory, we are *transformed into His Image.*

"As the teil tree, and as an oak, whose substance *is* in them when they cast *their leaves: so* shall the **Holy Seed** be the *substance* thereof" (Is. 6:13). In the fall and winter the oak tree holds on to its dead leaves until the *substance of life* within the tree, produces new buds to remove them; we, like the oak tree in type, are covered with dead and useless leaves—fit only for the fire—until the buds of life are reproduced in us by the Holy Spirit to remove them. "The leaves of the tree *were* for the healing of the nations" (Rev. 22:2). The new growth that buds forth in mankind, producing life—contains the power to heal the nations; because it is the Life of Christ within, as we express His Image in our earth.

Summary: Things are not always as they seem. God's purpose is always perfect in accomplishing His remarkable plan; and it is usually not in keeping with man's preconceived ideas—formed from a limited understanding. It is the deceiver's mission to block the illumination of truth from our understanding—it is the only means for the kingdom of darkness to continue the false reality of its existence—by blinding our minds. What the mind believes to be true becomes its seeming reality. The deceiver, referred to as the accuser of the brethren, began his deception with an accusation against God that continues to this present time—blaming God and us for his own evil intentions through deceptions that produce thoughts and actions that continue to thwart mankind. "My people are destroyed for lack of knowledge" (Hosea 4:6). We will continue to live in a false reality, as long as there is a lack of knowledge and understanding of the truth—until "the knowledge of the Glory of the Lord, covers the earth as the waters cover the sea (Hab. 2:14). As Jacob and Esau were separated from Rebekah's womb, we are to allow the Holy Spirit to work in us to separate the precious from the vile. "Therefore thus saith the Lord, if thou return, then will I bring thee again, *and* thou shalt stand before me: and if thou take forth the precious from the vile, thou shalt be as my mouth" (Jer.15:19). Obviously, if He has control of our mouth, He has the whole body. "If any man offend not in word, the same is a perfect man, *and* able also to bridle the whole body" (Jas.3:2). Judas hanged himself before the blood of Jesus was applied ***once and for all*** in the most Holy place, upon the Mercy Seat, not realizing the power of forgiveness and remission of sin through the Cross to remit his sin—when Jesus ascended to His Father. Paul, who was obviously, Jesus's chosen replacement for Judas, was apprehended under the blood covenant where his sin was remitted.

Chapter Four

God's Purpose for Jacob's Deception

In Defense of Jacob

Rebekah overheard Isaac speaking to his son Esau, asking him to go into the field to hunt for venison to make him the savory meat he loved and bring it to him so he could bless him before he died. Rebekah, having been told by the Lord that the elder was to serve the younger, being steadfast and obedient to what she had been told; quickly commanded Jacob to bring her two good kids of the goats, to be substituted for Esau's venison. "And Jacob said to Rebekah, his mother: Behold, Esau my brother *is* a hairy man and I *am* a smooth man; my father peradventure will feel me, and I will **seem** to him as a deceiver;...And Rebekah took goodly rainment of her eldest son Esau, which were with her in the house, and put them upon Jacob her younger son: and she put the skins of the kids of the goat upon his hands, and upon the smooth of his neck"... (Gen.27: 11.12.15.16).

Jacob **seeming** to be a deceiver was in fact, as his name indicates: a *supplanter.* Jesus came to earth as God born in the flesh—concealed within the mortal body of man, *wearing the disguise of mortal man in the same way Jacob wore the disguise of Esau*. Jacob's obedience in wearing animal skins, pretending to be Esau was necessary as a forerunner of Jesus Christ, granting the permission needed—making it possible for Jesus to come in the flesh of man—**seeming** to be a natural man, when He was in fact the Image of God *wearing the form of man*. Coming as the Son of man, birthed from a natural but virgin woman, as well as being the only begotten Son of God.

Jacob's act of obedience was a *necessary step of faith*, producing an agreement on earth—preparing the way, for Jesus Christ to enter the world as God in the flesh—*seeming*—to be a mortal man. Jacob's grandfather, Abraham before him, through faith and obedience offered his beloved son of promise: Isaac, preparing the way by supplying faith on earth for God to send His only begotten Son, as a sacrificial Lamb, offered to remit the sin of man—an action in the earth realm that produced faith in the heavens for God to manifest His purpose on earth. The Lamb caught in the thicket, represents Jesus—caught in the thicket of man's sin.

Man's choice against God's plan, produced thorns and thistles on earth, as a picture of his inward condition that has kept him snared in a *thicket of sin*, until Jesus became us so that we could become like Him. Faith, being the evidence of things not seen, is an unseen action that produces a visible manifestation on earth. Man's inward condition is seen in the conditions of *the world he has created,* as the *reflection of himself.*

Jacob's father Isaac, because of the dimness of his eyes did not discern him. When asked how he found the meat so quickly, he replied: *"because the Lord thy God brought it to me"* (Gen. 27:20). When she said to Jacob "obey my voice," Rebekah was speaking as an *oracle* of God, being obedient in fulfilling the things spoken to her by the Lord concerning her sons, a necessary participation on her part in reclaiming the blessing for mankind; through Jesus Christ. By *obeying* his mother's instructions, Jacob was *submitting to the will of God*, to prepare the way of the Lord.

"And Isaac said unto Jacob, Come near, I pray thee that I may feel thee, my son, whether thou *be* my very son Esau or not. And Jacob went near unto Isaac his father; and he felt him, and said, *The voice is Jacob's voice*, but the hands *are* the hands of Esau. And he discerned him not because his hands were hairy, as his brother, Esau's hands: so he blessed him" (Gen. 27:21-23). Like Jacob—Jesus's manner of speech was different than that of a natural man—since His appearance was that of a natural man—until He reached the age of thirty years, He was able to blend in—after His baptism, due to the changes in Him, brought about by the presence of the Holy Spirit, the differences that distinguished Him from other men became apparent.

Branded a Deceiver

Jacob feared that he would *seem* to be a deceiver; and so he has down through the ages. The misunderstanding concerning the importance of his actions in fulfilling what was required in the natural realm to precede the *spiritual* fulfillment, has been completely overlooked. This is an example of one of the less obvious gleanings from the field of His Word.

Isaac spoke of Jacob coming with **subtlety** and taking away his blessing. A type and shadow of what Jesus did, in coming to earth in the disguise of man to take back the blessing that was usurped through **subtlety** in the beginning. Jacob's action in getting the blessing from the natural man was necessary in preparing the way for Jesus, by granting the permission He needed to reclaim what had been lost through subtlety and deception that resulted in disobedience. Jacob's obedience to *his mother's instruction*—prepared the way for the *spiritual* fulfillment through Jesus Christ. Jacob was hesitant, not wanting to **seem** like a deceiver, but obeyed his mother. An interesting parallel: Jesus's ministry on earth began when He responded to *His mother's request,* He also hesitated—but submitted to His mother when He changed water into wine at the wedding feast in Cana. Like Jacob, He was embarking on a journey down an entirely new path. Both *submitted* to their *mother's instructions,* before a major change occurred in the direction of their paths.

When we recognize Jesus Christ as The Holy Seed of God, the only begotten Son of God, and receive the Holy Spirit as our only source of life through salvation, we enter into a spiritual battle zone where the natural man, like Esau—contests us for the territory he has held. Jacob had to flee from the face of Esau for the same reason God told Mary and Joseph to flee into Egypt to protect the young child from those who sought His life. Esau, true to his nature—like Cain before him—planned to *slay his brother* until God intervened through his mother and sent Jacob away. By sending Jacob away, Rebekah saved him from being slain—like Abel—by his brother's hand.

Rebekah spoke to Jacob: "Now therefore my son, *obey my voice;* and arise, flee thou to Laban, my brother to Haran and tarry with him *a few days* until thy brother's fury turn away" (Gen. 27:43). The reason she gave Isaac for sending Jacob away, was to prevent him from taking a wife from the daughters of Canaan, as Esau had done. Jacob's obedience to God, through his mother's instruction, was necessary in accomplishing God's purpose through him. A necessary step for all mankind in the path back to God—through the shed blood of Jesus Christ. As the Son of man, Jesus represents Adam and is called the second Adam, as the Son of God— The Seed of God, He could also be referred to as the second Abel.

Jesus Christ is the manifestation—the living reality, of all the types and shadows that represented God's chosen vessels in the Old Testament. He came to silence the cry of Abel's blood calling to God from the ground—a cry that brought judgment on the earth until *Jesus came to willingly offer* what had been *violently* taken away, *cancelling the debt of man,* through the forgiveness of sin.

God had to answer the cry of His own *Eternal Seed*—contained in the body of Abel, who was slain—calling to Him from the ground, where His life's blood was spilled; just as He answers it now when it calls to Him from our ground. It took many animal sacrifices; thousands of years and numerous covenants between God and man to secure enough acts of faith in the earth to produce an answer to that cry by sending His own Image in the form of man. The following poem contains a description of the searching and expectation of our souls for the manifest presence of God. It is the nature of our soul to seek and search for what it has lost—*never* to be satisfied with less. The soul is needy, and what we obtain we no longer need, so the search continues. The sense of dissatisfaction that we have all experienced, is our soul's awareness of a sense of loss—unaware of what that loss is, we try to fill the emptiness with *things* that can't satisfy, in an attempt to fill the void. It remains a puzzle, until we discover the missing piece of the puzzle that perfectly fits, to *complete* us. The soul can *never* be content with substitutes for what it has lost.

> Through the cold and lonely years,
> As I have wandered among men,
> Searching for a lost completion
> Through a blinding veil of sin,
>
> Somewhere in my deepest being
> Where no earthly eye can see
> Lay a quiet expectation:
> I knew you would come for me.

The Blessing Reclaimed

"And Isaac called Jacob and blessed him, and charged him, and said unto him: Thou shalt not take a wife of the daughters of Canaan" (Gen. 28:1.2). He was sent to the house of Bethel, his mother's father to take a wife from the daughters of Laban, his mother's brother. "*And God almighty bless thee,* and make thee fruitful, and multiply thee, that thou mayest be a multitude of people; and give the blessing of Abraham, to thee and to thy seed with thee; that thou mayest inherit the land wherein thou art a stranger, which God gave to Abraham" (Gen. 28:3.4). The

Holy Seed, within us is a stranger in our land—*body*, until our soul submits to God through the working of the Holy Spirit, to reclaim our rightful inheritance. The most important land we are to inherit and for our souls to reclaim dominion over, is our *body*, as we walk in the Spirit, and not in the flesh nature of the natural man.

The act of disobedience from the beginning, occurring first in the spirit realm, in Adam and Eve, then being re-enacted *visibly* in Cain's action against Abel; is a picture of man's separation from God. God used covenants and acts of obedience to reverse the sequence of events. Before an accomplishment in the spirit realm could transpire to bring man back to God, it was necessary for God to prove man's obedience—man had to prove his obedience through acts of faith. "Behold, to obey is better than sacrifice" (I Sam. 15:22).

Faith is stepping into an unknown and unfamiliar territory in an unseen realm. By faith, Abraham made a covenant with God to travel into an unknown and unfamiliar land in the natural realm, in obedience to God, believing and trusting in His willingness and ability to sustain him. The Old Testament is descriptive of God requiring man's obedience as proof of faith, sufficient to receive His greatest gift to man: His Son Jesus Christ. The way through the wilderness of disobedience within man, had to be **made straight**, through obedience. The Old Testament tells of many, who revealed their faith through their obedience—forerunners of Jesus Christ—culminating in John the Baptist. "He said, I *am* the voice of one crying in the wilderness, **Make straight** the way of the Lord, as said the prophet E-sai-as" [Isaiah] (John 1:23).

"As it is written in the book of the words of Isaiah the prophet, saying, the voice of one crying in the wilderness, prepare ye the way of the Lord, *make His paths straight.* Every valley shall be filled and every mountain and hill shall be brought low; and *the crooked shall be made straight,* and the rough ways shall be made smooth; and all flesh shall see the Salvation of God." (Luke 3:4-6). It took many acts of obedience to undo one act of disobedience. It has always been, and still is all about—The Seed of God, as seen in Abel and Jesus Christ, from Genesis to Revelation, from the beginning of creation to *the time of the restitution of all things.* Jesus Christ is the Salvation of God and *all* flesh shall see Him for who He is, and *through Him,* we shall see that we also are made in the Image of God. "When He shall appear, we shall be like Him; for we shall see Him as He is... because as He is, so are we in this world" (I Jn. 3:2-4:17). Created in the Image of God.

> As He is—so are we
> Created in His Image.
> An Immaculate Conception,
> Awaiting the resurrection,
> Of the new creation man
> To be revealed in us,
> As Sons of His Right Hand

An obvious example of man's willingness to obey God is seen in the unusual actions of Ezekiel that were a sign to Israel and a warning of God's judgment to come. "Thou also son of man, take thee a tile and lay it before thee, and portray upon it the city of Jerusalem and lay a siege against it, and build a fort against it… moreover, take thou unto thee an iron pan, and set it for a wall of iron between thee and the city: and set thy face against it, and it shall be besieged, thou shalt lay a siege against it. This shall be a sign to the house of Israel" (Ez. 4:1-3). Ezekiel's obedience to God forewarned Israel of His displeasure and the consequences to come.

There are many of Ezekiel's actions, recorded throughout the book of Ezekiel that *proved his faith* through his obedience—he was willing to humble himself regardless of how foolish he *appeared* to be. "But God hath chosen the foolish things of the world to confound the wise" (I Cor. 1:27). Ezekiel's actions surely fit the description of foolish things. He must have seemed like a child at play—appearing very foolish indeed to those observing his *many strange actions.*

Summary: God uses the natural and visible to portray the unseen and invisible for man's benefit. Jesus spoke in parables to relay meanings, making them more easily understood. As the heavens declare the glory of God—the earth has reflected and declared the condition of mankind since the beginning of time, when it was a thing of beauty reflecting the purity and beauty of God's masterpiece: man and woman in His Image. Man's fatal choice exchanged their beauty for ashes—and the earth became *a reflection of what they became*—bringing forth thorns and thistles. The visible, reflecting the invisible: the invisible being understood by the things that were *formed* to be visible from the creation of the world.

Chapter Five

Jacob's Ladder

"And Jacob went out from Beersheba and went toward Haran. And he lighted upon a certain place, and tarried there all night... And he dreamed, and behold, a ladder set upon the earth, and the top of it reached to heaven; and behold the angels of God ascending and descending on it. And, behold, the Lord stood above it, and said: I *am* the Lord God of Abraham thy father, and the God of Isaac: the land where on thou liest, to thee will I give it, and to thy seed" (Gen. 28:10-13).

Reference to "the land where on thou liest" obviously refers to the geographical location where he lay; however, it is also a *parable* and *type* of *his body* as an earthen vessel. "But we have this treasure [Seed of God] in earthen vessels, that the excellency of the power may be of God and not of us" (II Cor. 4:7). A greater understanding can be gleaned, by the awareness that man being formed from the earth as an earthen vessel, can be in type and shadow, likened to or synonymous with the earth *on* which he dwells; as well as referring to the actual geographical location he was lying on. Evidenced by the fact that our bodies consist of minerals that come from the earth from which we were formed—as well as containing comparable percentages of water and mass as the earth—it can be seen as an allegory of Jacob, as an earthen vessel, being the parcel of land the ladder was set upon. In addition to it referring to the actual land he was lying on.

When our soul is seeking for more of the presence of God, to be manifested in our lives, it's as if empowered by the Holy Spirit, we are climbing a ladder one rung at a time; how long we remain on one rung before going on to the next depends on our individual progress. There is no limit to how far we can climb until we reach the top. "And behold, the Lord stood above it" (Gen. 28:12) "... With men this is impossible; but with God all things are possible" (Matt. 19:26). The ladder with angels, ascending and descending, reaches into heaven between us and God—God works within the confines of our faith and trust in Him, as far as our *vision* and faith will carry us. "Where there is no vision, the people perish" (Prov. 29:18).

God does not force His will on us, but desires that we earnestly seek Him. It is mankind that sets limitations on God. His angels are ever present, ascending and descending, between heaven and earth, and are available to assist us in the completion of our spiritual journey to the Kingdom of God within us—to be reflected in our surroundings—as it was with Adam and Eve in the beginning.

May the Holy Spirit expound upon the Word, in ever increasing truth, until the Kingdom of God is visibly established in each one of us individually and collectively, as threads woven together in the tapestry of God—woven in His design with threads from the Tree of Life uniting us together as one in His Kingdom.

> Heaven and earth are longing
> To be woven together as one
> Threads of a lovely garment
> In the hands of the Holy One
>
> Weaving the threads together.
> Leaving the fragments behind,
> Completing an elegant garment,
> Woven in His design.

Only when heaven and earth are once again blended together as one, will we truly be free, and *completely* whole. "For since the beginning of the world *men* have not heard nor perceived by the ear, neither hath the eye seen, O God, beside thee, *what* He hath prepared for him that waiteth for Him" (Is. 64:4). "For God who commanded the light to shine out of darkness, hath shined *in* our hearts, to give the *light* of the *knowledge* of the glory of God in the face of Jesus Christ. (II Cor. 4:6).

When Jacob awakened, he said: "Surely the Lord is in this place; [in-him] and I knew it not… this is none other but the **house of God,** and this is the **gate of heaven**" (Gen. 28:16). Jacob suddenly awakened to the awareness of **his body being the house of God, and the Holy Seed within him—as being the gate of heaven.** He understood that the Seed of God within him was a ladder to God. "Know ye not that ye are the temple of God, and that the Spirit of God dwelleth in you?… for the temple of God is holy, which *temple* ye are" (II Cor. 3:16.17).

Rolling the Stone Away

When Jacob arrived in Haran, the land of his mother's brother, he saw a Well—with a great stone covering the mouth of the Well. "And it came to pass, when he saw Rachel the daughter of Laban, his mother's brother… that Jacob went near, and rolled the stone from the Well's mouth, and *watered the flock* of Laban his mother's brother" (Gen. 29:10). Jacob rolling the stone from the Well's mouth signifies and foreshadows, the Angel of the Lord rolling away the stone from the tomb—for Jesus, *the living water,* to come forth in *resurrection power* to give *living water to the flock of God.* "We are His people and the sheep of His pasture" (Ps. 100:3).

Jacob loved Rachel and agreed to serve her father Laban seven years for her. Jesus's love for our soul is in the truest form, what Jacob's love for Rachel represents to us. We see in the triangle of Jacob, Rachel and Leah, a picture of our relationship with God, in the outworking of the spiritual awakening in our souls.

Jacob, after serving seven years for Rachel to become his wife—discovered the next morning that Leah had been **substituted** for Rachel, "…and he said to Laban, **what is this thou hast done unto me**? did not I serve with thee for Rachel? Wherefore, then hast thou **beguiled me**?" (Gen. 29:25).

God spoke those very words to Eve when He approached them after they disobeyed Him and submitted themselves as servants to obey another. "And the Lord God said unto the woman, **What is this that thou hast done**? And the woman said the serpent **beguiled me** and I did eat" (Gen. 3:13). They **substituted** a seed of a lesser mortal existence that He hated, in the place of an Immortal Seed, whom He loved. "Yet I had planted thee a noble vine, wholly a right seed; how then art thou turned into the degenerate plant of a strange vine unto me?" (Jer. 2:21). A similar situation occurs when we invite Jesus into our lives and experience a relationship with Him, that can be compared to Rachel's first encounter with Jacob at the well. "And Jacob kissed Rachel, and lifted up his voice, and wept... and Jacob loved Rachel" (Gen. 29: 11.18).

In the beginning Adam and Eve were united in the love of God, until **they substituted** another in **His** place. We are the beloved of the Lord, as Rachel was the beloved of Jacob—yet Leah—who *in type* represents the unregenerate part of our soul—the first born, resurfaces within us to contest the new creation being formed in our soul. The Lord has to endure the unregenerate part of our soul for a time as Jacob did with Leah, until our whole soul is transformed by the renewing of our minds and heart, as the Holy Spirit enables the part of us that is the beloved of the Lord, to crowd out and overcome our old habits and desires.

The Wheat and the Soul

"And Laban said, it must not be so done in our country, to give the younger before the first born" (Gen. 29:26). We become a first born when we are born from the water of our mother's womb, in the flesh—the elder. When we receive salvation through Jesus Christ, we are born of the Spirit—the younger, through an Immaculate Conception, as the Holy Spirit moves upon the womb of our soul *with our consent.*

We have seen the two factions of the spirit in the Seed of God and the seed of man through Jacob and Esau, in the next chapter we will explore the facets of the soul, where choices are made, as we see the interaction between Rachel and Leah in the process of bringing forth the Seed promised to Abraham through Isaac and Jacob.

In (Psalms 34:2), David refers to his soul as her. "My soul shall make her boast in the Lord." Our soul can be compared to a bride whose bridegroom is he to whom she submits herself to obey. "Know ye not, that to whom ye yield yourselves servants to obey, his servants ye are to whom ye obey; whether of sin unto death, or obedience unto righteousness" (Rom. 6:16). It is time to: "...let the bridegroom go forth of His chamber, and the bride out of her closet" (Joel 2:16). The Seed of the Image of God is the true bridegroom of our soul—unless an unwise bride *chooses* to be united to the seed that causes man to sin—that resulted from deception.

Our souls operate very much like a womb—concepts sown in our thoughts, by the seed of the natural man or the Seed of the Image of God, are either rejected—or planted and nurtured until emotions and actions are born.

Our souls can be compared to wheat in Jesus's parable of the wheat and tares. "The field is the world; the good seed are the children of the kingdom; but the tares are the children of the wicked one" (Matt. 13:38). Jesus told His followers to let the wheat and the tares grow up together lest while they gather up the tares they would root up the wheat also, because tares look like wheat until the time of harvest, when they can be recognized for what they are. The tares represent the devil and his angels that the fire is prepared for. "Gather ye together first the tares, and bind them in bundles to burn them: but **gather the wheat into my barn**. [Wheat is threshed—but not burned] As therefore the **tares** are gathered and **burned in the fire;** so shall it be in the end of this world" (Matt. 13:30.40).

Evidence abounds all around us, attesting to signs that indicate the fullness of time—when iniquity is come to the full. A time when the tares begin to tower over the wheat, making their identity known—becoming visibly distinguished from the wheat—ushering in the end of this age and the time spoken of when "the kingdoms of this world are become the Kingdoms of our God and of His Christ, [when] He shall reign forever and ever" (Rev. 11:17). We are nearing the time when: "The earth shall be filled with the *knowledge of* the Glory of the Lord, as the waters cover the sea." (Hab. 2:14).

"The Son of man shall send forth His angels, and they shall gather out of His Kingdom all things that offend, [tares] and them which do iniquity; [chaff—result of wrong choices] and shall cast them into a furnace of fire: there shall be wailing and gnashing of teeth. Then shall the righteous [in each one of us] shine forth as the sun in the Kingdom of their Father. **Who hath ears to hear, let him hear**" (Matt. 13:41-43). Exactly what is it, He wants us to hear? God makes a division between the wheat and the tares—the Seed in us He loves and the parasite seed in us that He hates—the imposter that hates us and afflicts us body and soul. "Study to show thyself approved unto God, a workman that needeth not to be ashamed, **rightly dividing the word of truth**" (II Tim. 2:15). The Incorruptible Seed is approved unto God and need not be ashamed. It will not be pleasant to have the deeds of our flesh go up in flames; that is why we have been given the opportunity to be overcomers in this life. "And the very God of peace sanctify you ***wholly;*** and I pray God your ***whole spirit,*** and ***soul*** and ***body*** be preserved *blameless* unto the coming of our Lord Jesus Christ" (I Thess. 5:23).

The outer covering of the wheat is called the chaff: this coarse outer layer has no food value and is removed during the threshing process. The only purpose it has is, as a covering, until the time for its removal—when what can be shaken, will be shaken, and only things that cannot be shaken will remain. Being threshed will not be a pleasant experience, but it can be minimized when we cooperate with God and willingly offer up the chaff. Our resistance to God makes everything more difficult for us—by submitting to the man of sin—who cares *not* for our soul—instead of submitting ourselves to God, whose intentions toward us are more than honorable. "For I know the thoughts that I think toward you, saith the Lord, thoughts of peace, and not of evil, to give you an expected end" (Jer. 29:11). The chaff—covering on the wheat can be compared to the flesh covering us. We shed thousands of dead skin cells every hour; when we become full of light, with life, emanating from within us, we will be changed, having no more dead cells to shed, when death is swallowed up in victory, by the Seed of God that dwells within us.

"John answered, saying unto them all, I indeed baptize you with water; but one mightier than I cometh, the lachet of whose shoes I am not worthy to unloose: He shall baptize you with the Holy Ghost and with ***fire***: Whose fan *is* in His hand, and He will thoroughly purge His floor, and will ***gather the wheat*** into his garner; *but* the ***chaff He will burn*** with fire unquenchable" (Luke 3:16-17). <u>**We are not the chaff**</u>—the chaff is attached to our souls and the parasites are attached to the chaff, like mistletoe attaches to the outer bark of a tree, existing as a living entity, bearing poison berries, while draining the life from the tree—*but it is not the tree.* "Who shall dwell with the devouring fire? Who among us shall dwell with everlasting burnings? He that walketh righteously; and speaketh uprightly" (Is. 33:14.15). **The Holy Seed of God** planted in the beginning of creation **is who we are** and we are able (Abel) to dwell in the firey presence of a Holy God.

Surrounded by the chaff and surrounding the largest portion of the wheat is a coarse fiber called bran; it has food value and is good for cleansing the digestive system, to clear out the useless debris. It can be compared to the outer court of the temple—where sacrifices were made to atone for sin. Sin consists of all of the useless waste attached to the chaff on our soul. "But who may abide the day of His coming? And who shall stand when He appeareth? For He *is* like a refiners fire..." (Mal. 3:2). This portion of our soul is a *type* of Leah—her name means weak eyed, which indicates that she has limited vision and serves the flesh.

Surrounded by the bran the next layer of wheat is the gluten, the largest portion of the wheat, that has food value and can be ground into flour and made into a variety of desirable food products and served to others. This like the inner court of the temple—is a place of ministry and service to the people where they can be fed and nurtured. A type of Rachel, the beloved, who represents the new creation—the facet of our soul that has the *power of choice.* Her name means Ewe, a female sheep—she is the one who was tending the sheep when Jacob arrived in Haran. This represents the *contested portion of our soul*—the prize, the man of sin is after—the place of choice—where temptation occurs. In the beginning through subtlety he obtained the dominion on earth from Adam and Eve, but has been limited by not having *man's power of choice*. When man forfeited his God given dominion over the earth, by choosing to submit himself to obey the deceiver—he also lost his dominion over the body that was formed from the earth. Man retained the authority *to choose* whom he will serve, either the Holy Place in our soul where we are connected to the Seed of God or the part of our soul that is connected to and serves the flesh. We are continually presented with the *same subtle temptation* as Adam and Eve, so—*CHOOSE WISELY*—whom you will serve.

The most powerful and most nutritious portion of the wheat—the wheat germ, can be compared to the Holy Place where our soul, through the Holy Spirit, communes with God in the secret place—within the center of our innermost being, reserved for the Eternal Seed of the Most High God.

Summary: As previously noted in the first chapter, these references to Leah and Rachel are being used as parables to show the inner workings of the soul in mankind and are not limited to this one meaning—it is also a real historical account of their lives. Used in this context, shows how a substitution occurs after our first encounter with the Holy Spirit, when our humanity rises to the surface and has to be endured for a time, until Rachel the beloved one is able to *emerge in pre-eminence*. Jesus is listed in the first chapter of Matthew, as a descendant of Leah through the tribe of Judah—as the Son of Man— connecting Him to us in the realm of our humanity. As the

Son of God—our Shepherd is very protective—in the parable of the wheat and the tares, He emphasizes not confusing the wheat with the tares. "A bruised reed shall He not break, and the smoking flax shall He not quench: He shall bring forth judgment unto truth" (Is. 42:3). *Truth reveals His judgment against the tares within us—while rightly dividing—He protects His wheat.*

While pondering, what could be preventing God from ridding the earth of the man of sin? The thought occurred— the answer is found in the parable of the wheat and the tares. Man must recognize and realize that he has been living in a false reality concerning his identity—his *entanglement* with the tares has to be unraveled by the Word of Truth, in order to *separate* his false identity from his true reality, as the Seed of the Image of God. Until this occurs—to sling the enemy out of our land, would take the entangled soul along with it. "For thus saith the Lord: Behold I will sling out the inhabitants of the Land" [tares] (Jer. 10:18). The sword of the Spirit of Truth, has to divide the identity of the soul from the spirit of error, that has been produced through the alliance with the man of sin, who disguises himself to hide his actions, to blame us for his deeds—deeds that become our deeds, **only** when we *own* them, by making an alliance with, the man of sin to identify *ourselves* as the responsible parties. It is necessary that we separate ourselves from our false identity and embrace our true reality—then God will be able to pour out His fury upon the heathen (tares): "…for they have eaten up *Jacob*, and *devoured him*, and *consumed him*, and have *made his habitation desolate*." (Jer. 10:25). This scripture is referring to the Seed of the Image of God, represented in type by Jacob.

When His habitation within us is desolate, we are well aware of the emptiness of that desolation. Only the One, whose habitation we were created to be, can complete us, by filling in all of the empty places within us.

The burning of the wood hay and stubble and the works of the natural man will be consumed; but "He himself [*the part of our soul* likened to the wheat germ, that can follow no voice, but the Shepherds] shall be saved" (I Cor. 3:13). The largest and prized portion of our soul that retained the *power of choice*, represented by the gluten—83% of the wheat, is what the man of sin desires to obtain, he works through the most vulnerable part of our soul, comparable to the bran of the wheat—the superficial outer portion which leans toward serving the flesh. "And the very God of peace sanctify you *wholly* and I pray God your **whole** spirit and **soul** and body **be preserved** blameless unto the coming of our Lord Jesus Christ. Faithful is He that calleth you, who also will do it" (I Thess. 5: 23.24). The body and the Spirit are subject to the *choice* of our soul. We must not under value this *remaining* priceless *gift*—that we have retained in our possession, since the beginning of creation—*the power to choose* the salvation of our *whole soul*. Where the soul *chooses* to go the body and spirit follow. A diagram showing the comparison between the wheat and the soul can be seen at the end of the book.

A picture of our spiritual pilgrimage from darkness to light, from death to life, from Leah to Rachel can be further understood in the next chapter by the birth of Jacob's twelve sons and daughter.

Chapter Six

Fruitful and Barren

The births of Jacob's sons and daughter, also known as the children of Israel have names that are meaningful—describing their natures, as well as drawing a word picture describing what we experience in our walk of transforming faith.

Rachel, like Sarah and Rebekah before her, was barren, while Leah's womb was opened. "And Leah conceived, and bare a son, and she called his name **Reuben,**" [meaning, *see a son*] (Gen. 29:32). The meaning of his name can be comparable to our *seeing Jesus* as the Son of God, and receiving Him as *our Savior.*

She conceived again and called his name **Simeon,** which means *hearing.* After we recognize Jesus as the Son of God: "Faith cometh by hearing and *hearing* by the Word of God" (Rom. 10:17). Our faith increases as the Word is heard and received—to become flesh in us. The *quickening* we experience when the *Word of Truth is heard*—is the Seed of God within us—from the Holy place in our soul that is tuned in to God—witnessing to and responding in recognition to the truth. It is comparable to John the Baptist leaping in recognition in his mother's womb, when Mary entered Elizabeth's home with Jesus in her womb. "And it came to pass that, when Elizabeth *heard* the salutation of Mary, the babe leaped in her womb…" (Luke 1:41).

Leah conceived again, and bare another son and named him **Levi**, meaning **joined.** We first *see* the Son, receive faith through the *hearing* of the Word of God and then are *joined* to the Lord. The tribe of Levi was appointed by God as the priestly tribe—Jesus, being our Great High Priest. When we receive Jesus as our Savior and are reconciled to God, we are *joined*, to the Father through the Son, who sent the Holy Spirit to be our Comforter—to lead us into all truth.

Leah conceived again and bare a son, and she said, "Now will I praise the Lord, therefore she called his name **Judah**" [meaning **praise**] (Gen. 29: 35). We arrive at the place in our processing where we are filled with *praise* for so great a salvation. As we *praise* and give thanks, we become more aware of Him from whom all blessings flow. Leah left off bearing. The *first four* sons of Jacob represent the foundation of our salvation through faith.

Now begins the outworking between Leah and Rachel—between our old thoughts and habits and our desire to be transformed by the renewing of our minds. Here is where we are drawn into a place of conflict between two factions of the soul, and become aware that the battle lines have been drawn.

Jacob becoming angry when Rachel insisted that he give her children; said to her: "Am I in God's stead who hath withheld from thee the fruit of the womb? And she said behold my maid

Bilhah, go in unto her; and she shall bear upon my knees, that I may also have children by her" (Gen. 30:2.3). As Eve and Sarah before her, Rachel continues in the pattern of interference by suggesting that Jacob produce seed through her maid.

We see a repetition of Sarah's action, when she insisted that Abraham give her a child through her maid Hagar. It is a reoccurring pattern throughout the ages, as we attempt to accomplish by our own efforts what God alone can do to fulfill His promises to us, when in truth our *only* responsibility is our *response* to God's *ability*. Rachel's maid, Bilhah conceived and bore a son also.

"And Rachel said, God hath judged me, and hath also heard my voice, and hath given me a son. Therefore she called his name **Dan***"* [meaning **judging**] (Gen. 30:6). We have now entered into *judgment* for taking matters into our own hands, bringing judgment upon ourselves and sometimes others—as seen in the unfair judgment Joseph endured at the hand of his brothers.

If we toss judgment around—we had better duck—because boomerang! It will fly right back to us. With the same judgment we judge others we will be judged. "Judge not and ye shall not be judged: condemn not, and ye shall not be condemned: forgive, and ye shall be forgiven" (Luke 6:37). Let us not get caught in a perpetual cycle of strife by being encompassed with a boomerang of judgment—let us instead be encompassed with mercy—through the resurrection power of the Holy Spirit, where judgment is swallowed up in the victory of resurrection life. "Let us not therefore judge one another anymore: but judge this: rather that no man put a stumbling block or an occasion to fall in his brothers way, Let us therefore follow after the things which make for peace, and things wherewith one may edify another" (Rom. 14:13.19).

When Bilhah had a second son, Rachel said, "With great *wrestlings* have I wrestled with my sister, and I have prevailed: and she called his name Naphtali" (Gen. 30:8). The name **Naphtali,** means **wrestling.** She has now been instrumental in producing two additional brothers to conspire against the beloved son she was longing for. Cain *slew* Able—Ishmael *mocked* Isaac—Dan *judged* Joseph, and along with Naphtali, assisted their brothers in *wrestling* Joseph into a pit, eventually selling him to be a slave in Egypt. "Now we brethren, as Isaac was, are *the children of promise,* But as then he that was born after the flesh persecuted him *that was born* after the Spirit, even so *it is* now" (Gal. 4:28.29).

As Isaac was the son of promise, so do we as children of the promise, become the conduit for the Seed of the Image of God to be separated from the natural man, as Jacob was from Esau, to be brought to birth in us by the Immaculate Conception of the Holy Spirit.

The seed of the natural man will afflict our souls with confusion, doubts, unbelief and accusations to try to abort the Seed of God from coming to fruition—to prevent us from rising up within, to *reclaim* our rightful dominion. We are not often successful in a wrestling match with the natural man. We need to invite and rely on God's intervention: "Not by might, nor by power [ours], but by my Spirit, saith the Lord of Hosts" (Zech. 4:6). "For thus saith the Lord God, the Holy One of Israel; In returning and rest shall ye be saved, in quietness and in confidence [in God] shall be your strength..." (Is. 30:15).

When we *strike out* on our own to accomplish God's purpose in our own strength—that is exactly what we do—***strike out***.

When we put ourselves in a place of **judgment** a **wrestling** within our soul ensues. At this juncture, when we cry out to God for His intervention: Leah gives her maid to Jacob, and **Gad** is born, meaning a **troop cometh.** The Angels of the Lord of Hosts, are descending Jacob's ladder to assist us, as the battle within us rages; as the Seed of Jacob wrestles with the seed of Esau for dominion to be the life source *within* us—while Rachel and Leah contend for dominion to reproduce within our souls.

"And Zilpah, Leah's maid bare Jacob a second son. And Leah said, *Happy* am I, for the daughters will call me blessed: [indicating that she relied on and valued the opinion of others] and she called his name **Asher**" [meaning **happy**] (Gen: 30:13).

When we receive heavenly assistance from a troop of angels, we experience **happiness**—resulting in victory over the struggle with our self-efforts. It is a time when: "He gives us a little reviving in our bondage that a remnant might remain..." (Ezra 9:18).

"And Reuben went in the days of wheat harvest, and found mandrakes in the field, and brought them unto his mother Leah. Then Rachel said to Leah, give me I pray thee, of thy son's mandrakes. And she said unto her, is it a small matter that thou has taken my husband? And wouldest thou take away my son's mandrakes also? And Rachel said, therefore he shall lie with thee tonight for thy son's mandrakes" (Gen. 30:14.15). Leah was the intrusive one in Rachel and Jacob's relationship; yet she, as the usurper, accused Rachel of taking her husband—contesting for the special place that belongs to the beloved, chosen bride. Leah's reaction and attitude toward Rachel was one of resentment, even Rachel's ability to grant Leah time with Jacob, proved that Rachel was in control of their relationships and had the power to *choose* whether or not to bestow favor on Leah.

God hearkened to Leah, and she bare Jacob another son. Leah called his name **Issachar,** meaning a **hireling.** Rachel's lust for the mandrakes caused her to bargain with Leah in the same manner we bargain with the flesh to get what we want; she literally traded time with Jacob to Leah in exchange for mandrakes, a characteristic of the old nature—drawing the focus from God's purpose through the lust for gain. Her actions added one more jealous brother to gang up on Joseph. She was directly responsible for three out of ten of his tormentors, by taking matters into her own hands and *choosing* to satisfy her own will and desires.

Leah conceived again and bore **Zebulon,** his name means **dwelling.** God will allow us to *dwell* in the place where our lust has taken us for a time, and may even prosper us in this place to reveal what is in our hearts, and to prove if we truly desire Him and are committed to obey His will regardless of the cost; or if we like the *hireling* are committed only to what He can do to satisfy our lust for personal gain, through His gifts and graces.

Afterward, Leah bore a daughter Dinah, whose name means **judgment.** After a period of respite, the *hireling* must come under the light of God, to be *judged* and overcome through the power of the Holy Spirit at work in us. If we judge ourselves we need not be judged by another. "For if we judge ourselves, we should not be judged" (I Cor. 11:31).

God's judgment ended on the Cross—where it was exchanged for grace. Offered on the Mercy Seat—*blood bought mercy for mankind*, however, judgment still exists on earth as a *boomerang of perpetual e-motion* traversing from man to man, that has continued to encompass mankind for 2,000 years.

Jesus left us the key to our *own* judgment with these words: "Judge not and ye shall not be judged" (Luke 6:37). *We are the judges.* When we practice to judge, condemn or deceive, we are making a covenant and agreement to be judged, condemned and deceived. A seed sown—produces fruit after its own kind. The harvest of a seed sown, charts our path to success or failure, not only in a material sense, but most importantly our peace of mind and heart as well as our nature and character. What we sow outwardly, whether deception or truth, we are *making an alliance* with—to be produced inwardly.

A reality check is needed to understand the circumstances and happenings in our lives—consider this: what we are sending out into the lives of others, through our thoughts and deeds, is a *mirrored* image of what we are receiving into our own—mercy and forgiveness or judgment—rest or unrest—peace or anxiety—truth or deception. By carefully evaluating the image that is being mirrored back into our lives—we will be able to define and comprehend the cause and effect of the fruit we are bearing.

Life is not a random game of chance we are playing. There is always a cause for every *choice* and *action*—that results in an *effect* that becomes operative in our lives—whether for us or against us. "Say ye to the righteous that *it shall be well with him*. For they shall eat the *fruit of their doings*" (Is. 3:10). The consequences of judgment are built in as part of the package—once opened. The harvest of a seed sown charts our path "Either make the tree good, and his fruit good; or else make the tree corrupt, and his fruit corrupt: for the tree is known by his fruit" (Matt. 12:33). This scripture is a parable—making the comparison between man bearing fruit as a tree bears fruit. "...the fruit tree yielding fruit after his kind, whose seed is in itself..." (Gen. 1:11). *And so it is with man.*

There is much to be gleaned from this parallel between Rachel, who represents our soul, born of God, and Leah, who represents *in type* the part of us that continues in the old habits born of the flesh. The soul joined to the Lord, submits to His processing as we walk from darkness into the light of truth; not always choosing wisely—yet *eager to learn* from our wrong choices; sometimes being deceived—yet *eager to repent* and receive correction, as our Lord opens our eyes to see the error of our ways. His Life is reproduced in the true identity of our soul, the beloved of the Lord, comparable to Rachel and her relationship with Jacob.

Adding

"And God remembered Rachel, and God hearkened to her, and opened her womb" (Gen. 30:22). Through much preparation along with many trials, errors and much travail, our soul is now ready to produce fruit unto the Lord. "And she conceived, and bare a son: and said, God hath taken away my reproach: And she called his name Joseph; and said: The Lord shall add to me another son" (Gen. 30:23.24). The name *Joseph* means *adding*—his very name was an act of faith on Rachel's part to produce another son.

"And Israel said unto Joseph… God shall be with you, and bring you again unto the land of your fathers. Moreover, I have given to thee one portion above thy brethren" (Gen. 48:21.22). His father blessed him with the blessings of heaven above and the earth beneath.

> One portion for each son of Jacob
> A part for each heir of the Lord;
> Inheritance promised the Father,
> Will come to the sons through His Word.
>
> But in Joseph—the joy of his father,
> Born with his mother's heart,
> Heaven and earth are united
> Adding to Joseph, a double part.

Summary: We are brought back to the beginning when the **I Am that I Am, added** an extension of Himself in—**Ad+Am=Adam**—created to be the habitation of the most high God, before Adam chose to add another extension to himself through his disobedience. God *subtracted* when He destroyed the double portion of Cain by sending the flood, and *added* when He gave a double portion to Joseph through his father. God always keeps His books balanced. Another example of this is when He chose to transform Saul of Tarsus, through the redemption of the shed blood of Jesus, giving him a new nature, bringing life to God's dormant Seed that was in him, and renaming the new creation: Paul—a replacement for

Judas—whose natural man was just as depraved as Judas—the one He was replacing. Jesus, a sinless Lamb atoned for the loss of Abel a sinless lamb. An eye for an eye. Saul, an accomplice to the murder of God's people—through redemption—replaced Judas a thief, an accomplice to the crucifixion of God's Son. How can anyone possibly believe the accusation—planted by the deceiver in their thoughts—daring to suggest they are unworthy of redemption through Jesus Christ, with such an example as this? We are *all* born in sin through Adam—we have *all* been *redeemed* through Jesus Christ.

Chapter Seven

Ringstraked, Speckled and Spotted

When Jacob sought to be released from his service to Laban, he was coaxed to remain with him for wages. Jacob set his own price: "I will pass through thy flock today, removing from thence all the speckled and spotted cattle, and all the brown cattle among the sheep, and the spotted and speckled among the goats; and of such shall be my hire" (Gen. 30:32).

Jacob fed the flocks of Laban, according to their agreement. "And Jacob took him rods of green poplar, and of the hazel and chestnut tree; and pilled white strakes in them, and made the white appear which *was* in the rods. [In modern English: He peeled a portion of bark off the rods to make white streaks in them] And he set the rods which he had pilled before the flocks in the gutters of the watering troughs when the flocks came to drink that they should conceive when they came to drink. And the flocks conceived before the rods and brought forth cattle; ringstraked, speckled, and spotted" (Gen 30:37-39).

Notice that he set the rods in the gutters of the watering trough. Our society today has accepted as normal that which in past generations was considered shocking and on the gutter level. It appears that without God's intervention in the current state of affairs, we could all become ringstraked, speckled, and spotted by the influences we are exposed to in the world around us. "And except those days be shortened there should no flesh be saved: but for the elects sake those days shall be shortened" (Matt. 24:22). The elect is the Seed of God in every man. It may be dormant or in various stages of awakening, but it is there—for it cannot die—because in it is everlasting life. He is coming for "a **glorious church**, not having spot or wrinkle, or any such thing: but that it should be holy and **without blemish**" [not ringstraked, speckled and spotted] (Eph. 5:27).

Our souls are weak and limited, when united to the natural man, who is subject to the man of sin, that *dominates* our soul. When we exercise our *power of choice* and choose to be united to the Spirit of the *living* God, we who were once ringstraked, speckeled and spotted by the man of sin, are cleansed from the spots and wrinkles he has produced—our souls become *stronger*, as we are led into truth, by the Spirit of Truth. God set the *strength* of the Seed of His Image—in our ringstraked, speckeled and spotted humanity. Jacob set the rods before the *stronger* cattle of Laban's flocks and increased exceedingly. The process Jacob used to create the desired result is a powerful statement of how things we are exposed to in our lives are being imprinted within us having a *strong influence* on what we produce. What we see and hear has a tremendous impact on us, especially during our formative years. When our focus is on the *strength* Jesus made available to us, instead of the weakness of the flesh, old things begin to pass away and all things become new. "For the invisible things of Him from the creation of the world are clearly seen, being understood by the things that are made" (Rom. 1:20). The computer is an excellent example of the things that are made—reflecting the complexities of humanity. A parallel can be seen between the two. It reflects and reveals how we are imprinted and programed by our environment and our responses to it.

A computer has a motherboard—the main circuit board that holds the central processing unit and regulates the function of the different components of the computer. The central processing unit is the brain that is plugged into the motherboard. The motherboard works like a spinal cord that distributes information to and from the central processing unit.

We have an inner computer that works much the same way. The Holy Seed containing the nature, character and Image of God, planted in mankind at creation, is plugged into the Holy Spirit that distributes information to our soul from the Image of God in Christ, who is our *central processing* unit within; and can be compared to the Father and the Son—the mind of Christ—while the *motherboard* clearly depicts the function of the Holy Spirit.

The computer operates in accordance with what is programed into it, we are programed from birth by what society, education and our environment imprints within us; as well as the genetics we are born with. The story of our life is written within us—filed away in our personal computer. The Book of Revelation speaks of the books being opened before the throne of God. We *are the books* that are to be opened and everything concerning us is imprinted within us. We can be compared to

E-books that are printed off the computer. Another example of invisible things being clearly seen by things that are made.

Visions of an enormous library somewhere in the sky, containing books that record and reveal our lives, is a parable and an allegory—that can be compared to a computer printout—representing *what we contain within ourselves.* "And I saw the dead, small and great, stand before God; and the books were opened; and another book was opened, which is the *book of life*: and the dead were judged out of those things which were written in the books, according to their works" (Rev. 20:12). We contain both the book of life imprinted within the Seed of God, as well as the book containing the record of the deeds done in the body, according to the choices we have made as to whom we will serve. In near death experiences, when a person sees their life passing before them, it is coming from the inside of them, and being projected into their minds eye. Be aware that whatever we see, hear, think, whatever we say and whatever we do is being imprinted and recorded within us. Since we are being recorded from within—apparently we are all on hidden camera. It also appears that God created the first personal computer in Adam. Another example of the pre-existence of things, that God inspired or allowed man to discover.

You Are More Than You Realize

"A *Seed* shall serve Him; it shall be accounted to the Lord for *a generation,*" [His Incorruptible Seed] (Ps. 22:30). "Verily I say unto you, this **generation** shall not pass, till all these things be fulfilled" (Matt. 24:34). "But ye *are* a **chosen generation,** a royal priesthood, an holy nation, a peculiar people; that ye should shew forth the praises of Him who hath called you out of darkness into His marvelous light" (I Peter 2:9). His Seed is an *eternal generation* without end.

"Let no man deceive you by any means: *for that day* [day of Christ] *shall not come*, except there come a falling away first, and that man of sin, be revealed, the son of perdition; who opposes and exalts himself above all that is called God or that is worshipped; so that he as god sitteth in the temple of God showing himself that he is god" (II Thess.2:3.4). A clear description of the imposter that has stolen our identity.

Since our bodies are the temple of God, this is describing the seed of disobedience—the man of sin—typified by Cain and Esau sitting within us causing us to sin. There are a lot of things in our bodies that are not in our hearts. We need to recognize our true identity and separate ourselves from the enemy of our soul that sits in our temple *pretending to be us—he is not us and we are not him*. Our bodies are the temple that the man of sin sits in. The temple is holy and was made to be inhabited by a Holy Seed containing the very Image of God, our true identity; the Kingdom of God within us.

"And now ye know what **withholdeth** that he may be revealed in his time. For the mystery of iniquity doeth already work: only he who now letteth **will let,** until he be taken out of the way. And then shall that wicked be revealed, whom the Lord will *consume with the spirit of His mouth* and shall destroy with the brightness of His coming" (II Thess.2:6.7). It is imperative that we understand—the seed of disobedience working through the natural man and the thoughts he projects, is an enemy to our souls, and as long as we are deceived into believing we are him and he is us—that deception is **withholding** us from our true purpose and destiny. It is our lack of knowledge of the truth that **will let** this iniquity work in us.

There is no mystery when the truth is revealed. When the *light of truth* uncovers the hiding place of the man of sin—the mystery of iniquity vanishes like smoke in the wind—because he can only exist through his nature and character of lies and deception. "Because ye [the man of sin] have said, We have made a *covenant with death*, and with hell are we at agreement; when the overflowing scourge shall pass through, it shall not come unto us: for we have made lies our refuge, and under false-hood have we *hid* ourselves: [these words expose the conspiracy against every soul—a conspiracy that leaves the soul to bear the consequences of actions hatched in iniquity by the man of sin]. Therefore thus saith the Lord God…Judgement also will I lay to the line, and righteousness to the plummet: and the hail shall sweep away the refuge of lies, and the waters shall overflow the hiding place. [when the living water flows from our innermost being the refuge of lies will be swept away] And your covenant with death shall be disannulled, and *your agreement with hell* shall not stand; when the overflowing scourge shall pass through, then ye [the man of sin] shall be trodden down by it" (Is. 28:14-18).

This scripture describes the enemy of our soul that sits in our temple lording over us by blinding us through deception. The mystery of iniquity is at work in us, because our soul in bondage to the man of sin sitting in our temple, **will let** iniquity work, until the truth concerning this son of perdition is revealed; who **withholdeth** truth from us—to prevent us from understanding the truth of our identity. Our bondage will *allow* or *let* this iniquity work until this imposter is revealed, and is consumed by the Spirit of the Lord's mouth, which is the Word of Truth; and by the *brightness* of His coming—as the eyes of our understanding are opened and we are *illuminated* from within to receive the truth of our being.

When we are able to discern the reality of our identity as the Seed of God, we will also be able to identify the usurper who sits in our temple claiming to be us, the one who says: "I will ascend into heaven I will exalt my throne above the stars of God… Yet thou shalt be brought down to hell, to the sides of the pit. They that *see* thee shall narrowly look upon thee, and consider thee, saying, is this, the man that made the earth to tremble, that did shake kingdoms? That made the world as a wilderness, and destroyed the cities thereof; that opened not the house of his prisoners?" (Is. 12: 13-16). Our souls are prisoners—held captive by the man of sin, until our eyes are opened to discern the whole truth of our identity and our complete redemption through Jesus Christ. It is time for us to recognize and prevent the man of sin from misappropriating, misusing and abusing us body and soul. He is contesting us for his very existence—a parasite cannot survive without a host—it is time for us to quit hosting our own destruction—by allowing the outside in; when we should be seeking and allowing the Seed of the Image of God to work from the inside out. We are gently drawn from our *innermost* being—where the living water flows from the love of God, while we are being pulled, pushed, lured and tempted from the outside in, by an *identity thief.*

It is important that we recognize who we *really are,* and it is just as necessary that we understand *who we aren't.* When the scales are removed from our eyes, and we see the truth of the matter; we will also narrowly look upon and consider saying: "is this the man that made the earth to tremble, that did shake kingdoms?" When we become aware that it is the man of sin that has *sat* in our temple—*claiming to be us*—when in fact it is a usurper that has deceived us, by invading our thoughts, causing us to err—the truth will open our prison doors. As it was in the beginning, so it is now, until the eyes of our understanding are opened to receive the truth of our being: an understanding that evaded Adam and Eve or they would not have chosen against themselves, putting not only themselves but all of creation into bondage.

God created man to be the habitation of His Spirit. When man was deceived and usurped, what God had planned to inhabit, was invaded by another seed that was alienated from all that is of God. "Whosoever is born of God *doth not commit sin*: for **His Seed** remaineth in him and **he cannot sin, because he is born of God**" (I John 3: 9). The Incorruptible Seed does not corrupt nor can it be corrupted. "… Whosoever doeth not righteousness is not of God" (I John 3: 10). There are *two entirely different seeds* housed in one lump of clay, made in the likeness of Adam and Eve. The pattern created in heaven, became altered on earth by their fatal choice. Through Jesus Christ, by an Immaculate Conception of the Holy Spirit, we can be born anew, of a Seed that does not sin—after the original pattern in heaven—as was intended for us from the beginning of God's creation.

Wrestling for a Blessing

As Jacob was returning to his father's house before he encountered Esau in the flesh, he wrestled with a man until

the breaking of day. Though the hollow of his thigh was out
of joint, he refused to cease his wrestling until he received a
blessing. "And he said unto him thy name shall no more be
called Jacob, but Israel; [he received a new name for a new
nature] for as a prince hast thou power with God and men,
and hast prevailed" (Gen. 32:28). Jacob won the battle in the
spirit realm and prevailed so that when he encountered Esau he
stood before him victorious. The battle was the Lord's won by
His Spirit. "Not by might, not by power but by my Spirit, saith
the Lord of Hosts" (Zech. 4:6).

Jacob through the Seed of God in him, by the power of God,
had to wrestle down the man of sin, the son of perdition in his
own temple before he could stand before Esau without fear, as a
prince prevailing with God and man. The affliction in his flesh
in the hollow of his thigh was a sign that his flesh had suffered
defeat, while the Seed of God in him was victorious. "And Esau
ran to meet him, and embraced him, and fell on his neck, and
kissed him; and they wept" (Gen. 33:3).

This miraculous peaceful reunion between Jacob and Esau
was the result of Jacob's victory over his flesh. The victory
gained by the Spirit was then manifested in the natural realm,
as Jacob overcame through the power contained in the Holy
Seed within him. It was then he was able to say: "I have seen
God face to face, and my life is preserved" (Gen 33:30). Man
cannot see his face and live, refers to the *abdication of the man
of sin*, when the Holy Seed of God's planting, is revealed in
us—then like Jacob, our souls will behold God face to face—
His face reflecting in our own—through His Seed within us.
"For the terrible one is brought to nought, and the scorner is
consumed, and all that watch for iniquity are cut off. They also

that erred in spirit shall come to understanding, and they [our souls] that murmured shall learn doctrine" (Is. 29:20.21).

> The potter, the shaper, the forger my friend
> Drawing the gold from contemptible blend.
> Out of the oven and into the wind.
> Only my Lord knows the end.
>
> Earthbound and airborne, faithful and stray,
> Living while dying—O Father the way,
> Is steep and It's narrow and I'm made of clay
> Stay with me Lord all the way.
>
> Out of duality, out of the pain
> Of pieces and patches of Abel and Cain,
> No more Esau wearing my name,
> Only God's Seed—will remain.

The Son of the Right Hand Foreshadowed

Rachel had stolen her father's images, and hidden them. Jacob being *unaware that Rachel had taken them*, when pursued and accused said: "With whomsoever thou findest thy gods, *let him not live*" (Gen. 31:32). These words were spoken before Rachel's travail to bring forth her second son. "And they journeyed from Bethel; and there was but a little way to come to Ephrath: [which is *Bethlehem*] and Rachel travailed, and she had hard labor And it came to pass, when she was in hard labor, that the midwife said unto her, fear not: thou shalt have this son also. And it came to pass, as her soul was departing [it was decreed that she could not live—because of Jacob's word against whoever had stolen Laban's god's]… that she called his name Benomi: [which means; the son of my sorrow], but his father called him **Benjamin"** [*the son of the right hand*] (Gen. 35:16-18).

"And Joseph also went up from Galilee, out of the city of Nazareth into Judaea unto the city of David which is called *Bethlehem*… And so it was, that, while they were there the days were accomplished that she [Mary] should be delivered. And she brought forth her firstborn son" (Luke 2:4.6.7). Benjamin and Jesus were both born in *Bethlehem*, and both are called the Son of the right hand.

As Rachel's soul was departing, she named her second son Benomi—the son of my sorrows. Another time, another place, another *mother* stood at the foot of a Cross and travailed for the Son of her sorrows. A Son, also called by *His* Father: The Son of the Right Hand. The fulfillment of this type and shadow portrayed at the birth of Benjamin is seen in the birth, death, burial and resurrection of Jesus Christ—the perfect sinless sacrifice—who freely became the Son of sorrows in our behalf. Benjamin, being called by his father, the son of the right hand, was foreshadowing Jesus—seated at the right hand of His Father. Jesus, "Who being the brightness of His glory, and the Express Image of His Person, and upholding all things by the Word of His power, when He had by Himself purged our sins, sat down on the *right hand* of the Majesty on high" (Heb. 1:3).

Jesus is the fulfillment of what Benjamin foreshadowed, just as He is the fulfillment of the entire Old Testament, whether hidden or obvious within its pages. The whole purpose was to prepare the way for His coming: just as He prepared the way for the Holy Spirit to be accepted on earth, so the Holy Spirit could prepare the way for His returning by leading us into all truth. The Son of the Right Hand is the visible portrayal of God's Seed in man. His Word says that He sets the sheep on *His right hand* and we as His people are the sheep of His pasture—also created to be on the *right hand* of God.

Summary: It has always been about Christ and His Image being formed in mankind. All was portrayed in the natural realm before He was openly manifested as Jesus Christ: The Son of the Right Hand. Many have eyes to see and ears to hear, but they hear not, nor do they see the work of the Holy Spirit in their midst; just as they closed their eyes and ears and hardened their hearts, two thousand years ago when Jesus walked among them—from infancy to the Cross—to be seated on the right hand of God. The Holy Spirit walks within and among those today, who *willing allow* the Spirit access, to open their eyes and ears of understanding and transform their lives. We have the *choice* to classify ourselves as sheep on the right hand of God and live in His glorious light or choose to identify ourselves with the goats on His left.

In the dream Jacob had while fleeing from the wrath of his brother Esau, he saw a ladder that reached from earth to heaven—where God stood above it—with angels ascending and descending between earth and heaven. The dream occurred while he was on his way to Haran to seek a bride—where he found more than he bargained for, when Leah was substituted for Rachel his chosen bride.

The children born to Leah and her maid, along with those born to Rachel and her maid, who made up the house of Israel, were given meaningful names that describe the progression in our quest for God. When Jesus died on the Cross, the veil in the temple was rent, removing the separation between God and man. When he offered His blood on the mercy seat—the wall of partition separating heaven from earth was torn down—making the way for heaven and earth to be united and woven together as one.

Each rung on the ladder in Jacob's dream that leads us to God can in type represent each of the sons of Jacob. Beginning on the first step with Reuben whose name means—see a son—ending on the twelfth step with Be-no-ni—the son of sorrows, who was renamed Benjamin the Son of the Right Hand. Each step revealed in the previous chapter-six, portrays the path of our spiritual journey to illumination and enlightenment as we are led into truth by the Holy Spirit, until we reach the goal of entering into His rest that was prepared for us from the beginning of creation.

The cycle is complete in our walk with Jacob's sons and daughter, when the son of sorrows is swallowed up in victory, by the son of the right hand. When Benjamin—the son of the right hand came forth, it was preceded by a loss of life to the natural flesh, as it was with Rachel's death when Benjamin was born. Jacob unknowingly sent out a decree against one whom he loved when he said that whoever stole Laban's images: let him die.

A decree of condemnation was sent out when Adam and Eve chose against life, after being told that by eating of the tree of the knowledge of good and evil they would die. *God had to allow those whom he loved to die,* because they *chose* death. *He also had to allow Jesus, whom he loved, to die on the Cross* so that we could be redeemed—to be sons of the right hand and no longer sons of sorrow. We were crucified with Christ, *His death counting as our own.* "For if we have been planted together in the likeness of His death we shall be also in the likeness of His resurrection. Knowing this that our old man is crucified with Him… **For he that is dead is freed from sin**. Likewise reckon ye also yourselves to be dead indeed unto sin, but alive unto God through Jesus Christ our Lord" (Rom. 6:5-6.11).

Chapter Eight

Redemption through His Blood

Abel's blood was shed ***without his consent,*** as a lamb slain—portraying visibly the lamb slain in the spirit realm by his parent's disobedience: bringing the whole creation under judgment. Jesus brought redemption through His blood, ***with His consent,*** taking away judgment through the forgiveness of sin. When He said "Father, forgive them; for they know not what they do" (Luke 23:34), it was true concerning all mankind then and from that time forth—His forgiveness—covering us all.

When the earth produced thorns and thistles in response to the *choice* made by Adam and Eve, it was a reflection of their inward condition—they produced a strange vine that was *not* of God's planting. No longer was the garden of God, manifested in them or reflected in their surroundings.

God's judgment—the effect, due to sin—the cause, is seen throughout the Old Testament. The need for the continual offering of animal sacrifices was due to the blood of Abel, crying out to God from the ground. Jesus came in the visible form of man to cleanse the land of the shed blood of righteous

Abel—coming as an answer to what the cry of Abel's blood signified, as the visible portrayal of the shedding of the blood of the Lamb, slain from the foundation of the world in Adam and Eve—Jesus willingly offered, as an atonement, His own sinless blood—once and for all.

Cleansing the Land

"And to Jesus the mediator of the new covenant, and to the blood of sprinkling [on the Mercy Seat] *that speaketh better things than that of Abel*" (Heb. 12:24)...."for blood it defileth the land: and **the land cannot be cleansed of the blood that is shed therein, but by the blood of him that shed it"** (Num. 35:33). This was a law and *had to be fulfilled.* Jesus came to fulfill all of the law, making it of none effect, by replacing it with the Law of the Spirit of Life: making us free from the law of sin and death.

Jesus's offering was twofold: coming as the Son of God, in answer to the cry of Abel's blood, and as the Son of Man, in answer to man's need for redemption, through His blood. The Son of God came in an earthen vessel, wearing the disguise of a natural man, as Jacob did before Him when he pretended to be Esau. He who knew no sin, came in the likeness of sinful flesh as the Son of Man, and willingly took all sin upon His own body and shed His innocent blood to atone for all sin. Jesus, like Abel before Him, was the Seed of God, a Lamb without spot or blemish.

Under the law, an offering for sin had to be a male lamb without spot or blemish. An eye for an eye—Jesus as a sinless Lamb was atoning for the loss of a sinless Lamb; a price that had to be paid. Abel, an innocent *unwilling* Lamb—was sacrificed for Adam and Eve because sin entered the world. Their *disobedience* resulted in them birthing the **seed of disobedience** in Cain—who slew Able. Jesus, a *willing* Lamb was sacrificed for the shedding of Abel's innocent blood, as well as atoning for *all* sin from the time of its *inception* until the *Cross*—where sin was *terminated*—when the innocent blood of a willing Lamb washed it all away.

The judgment of death was on us all, until He freely gave His life canceling out judgment by exchanging death for life through mercy: reversing the choice of Adam and Eve, who exchanged their life for death through deception that produced disobedience.

Since, according to the law, the land could only be cleansed of the blood that was shed in it by the one who shed it, as the Son of Man; **Jesus cleansed the land of the blood that was shed in it—by coming in the flesh—assuming the identity of the one who shed it,** offering His own blood for the redemption of **all mankind.**

"For as in Adam **all** died, even so in Christ shall **all** be **made alive. But every man in his own order;** Christ the first fruits: afterward **they that are Christ's at His coming**" (I Cor. 15:23). The **first fruits** are those who **hear** and **believe without seeing.** Since all are **made** alive**, they who are Christ's at His coming,** refers to those who see and are left with no other option than to believe what can no longer be denied, when all shadows of doubt have been erased by the fire of His presence at His coming. "Jesus saith unto him, Thomas, because thou hast seen me thou hast believed; blessed are they that have *not seen*, and *yet* have believed" (John 20:29).

Revealed by Fire

"A fire goeth before Him, and burneth up His enemies round about. His lightnings enlightened the world; the earth saw and trembled. The hills melted like wax at the presence of the Lord of the whole earth" (Ps. 97:3). "Everyman's work shall be made manifest: for the day shall declare it, because it shall be *revealed by fire*; and the fire shall try every man's work of what sort it is. If any man's work, abide which he hath built thereupon, he shall receive a reward. [first-fruits] If any man's work shall be burned he shall **suffer** loss: but **he himself shall be saved**; *yet so by fire*" [those who are Christ's at His coming] "Know ye not that ye are the temple of God and that the Spirit of God dwells within you?" (I Cor. 3:13-16). "For our **God is a consuming fire**" (Heb.12:29).

"But now thus saith the Lord that created thee O *Jacob,* and He that formed thee O Israel, fear not: for I have redeemed thee, I have *called* thee by thy name, thou art mine... **When thou walkest through fire thou shalt not be burned; neither shall the flame kindle upon thee**" (Is. 43:1-2). The witness to the truth of these words is verified in the book of Daniel, when Nebuchadnezzar commanded his mightiest men to bind Shadrach, Meshach, and Abednego and cast them into a fiery furnace. "And the princes, governors and captains, and the king's counselors, being gathered together, saw these men, upon whose bodies the fire had no power, nor was an hair of the head singed, neither were their coats changed, nor the smell of fire had passed on them" (Dan. 3:27).

When we stand before God, only that which can withstand the fire of His presence will remain; "... but he himself shall be saved; *yet so by fire*" (I Cor. 3:15). This scripture makes reference to the Seed of God and His Life in the soul that was activated by the breath of God that cannot perish. *A fireproof, Incorruptible Seed*—only the works of the natural man—the tares and the chaff will be consumed, as is shown in the parable of the wheat and the tares, when the wheat is separated into His barn to be threshed, while the tares are bound in bundles to be burned. We shall all experience a shaking on the threshing floor to separate the wheat from the chaff, until only what *cannot* be shaken, will remain. "Whose fan is in His hand, and He will thoroughly purge His floor, and gather His wheat into the garner; but *He will burn up the chaff with unquenchable fire*" (Matt. 3:12).

Jesus said: "I am come to send fire [Holy Spirit] on the earth; and what will I, if it be already kindled?" (Luke 12:49). "…And under His Glory He shall kindle a burning like the burning of a fire. And the light of Israel shall be for a fire, and the *Holy One for a flame*: [His Seed within us is an eternal flame—lit by the fire of His Glory], it shall *burn* and devour his *thorns* and his *briers* in one day" (Is. 10:16.17).

> There is in Christ a continual burning,
> Love that consists of an unending fire.
> In Him we find that our heart's deepest yearnings
> Pass through the flames of His will and desire.
>
> Who can abide in the fire of His presence?
> Who can remain when His love is the test?
> The soul, He protects, as His love never lessens:
> His child, He has drawn to the warmth of His breast.

"For thou wilt not leave my soul in hell: neither wilt thou suffer thy **Holy One** to see corruption" (Ps. 16:10). Corruption will melt away in His presence. All that will remain is His **Incorruptible Seed** and its fruit. The Incorruptible Seed, born of the Spirit of God is fireproof. We have heard testimonies from those who have experienced hell, either in visions or near death experiences. Here is a thought worth pondering: could it be possible *in some cases*, the seed of the natural man—who submits to, and serves the man of sin—aka the antichrist, among other names, is greeted in visions or after death by those spirits to whom he has yielded himself as a servant to obey while on earth, and is tormented for a time by those spirits of darkness that have hidden within him, usurping his true identity? Each of these testimonies, have one common denominator, the soul cries out to God—even those who have not believed God existed—causing the spirits of darkness to vanish. His ear is always open to hear the cry of His Seed in man. "He shall call upon me and I will answer him" (Ps. 91:15). Verifying the word that **every** knee shall bow and every tongue confess that Jesus is Lord; to the Glory of God our Father.

"And this shall be the plague wherewith the Lord will smite all the people that have fought against Jerusalem; their flesh shall consume away while they stand on their feet, and their eyes shall consume away in their holes, and their tongue shall consume away in their mouth" (Zech. 14:12). Zechariah's prophetic utterance concerning Jerusalem speaks of those who *oppose their own souls* by fighting against their only true reality—the Seed of God within them. The spirits that cause the people to err are antichrist spirits, whose objective is to kill—steal and to destroy, to keep us from realizing the truth of our identity. They care not for souls that are precious to God. Their mission is to use whatever means necessary, to over-ride man's will; God will not over-ride man's will by using force, to take what is not *freely* given.

There is a Spiritual Israel, that which **Is-real,** that is typified by natural Israel. The New Jerusalem is a type of the Bride of Christ, which represents our soul submitted obediently to God, as a bride to her husband. God will also defend the natural Jerusalem—which is a *type* of the Heavenly Jerusalem. "And I John saw the holy city, New Jerusalem, coming down from God out of heaven, prepared as a bride adorned for her husband. And I heard a great voice out of heaven saying, Behold the tabernacle of God *is* with men, and He will dwell with them, and they shall be His people, and God Himself shall be with them, *and be* their God" (Rev. 21:2.3). This is a description of the invisible Heavenly Jerusalem becoming visible within us—clothing us with our bridal adornment *from within,* and being reflected in our surroundings.

"Little children, it is the last time: and as ye have heard that antichrist shall come, even now are there *many* antichrists, whereby we know that it is the last time" (I John 2:18). All that opposes Christ is antichrist—it is the vessel of dishonor that dwells in our lump of clay. "He that is not with me is against me" (Matt. 12:30). The word against means to oppose, the word antichrist means an opponent of Christ. We are all guilty before we come to know Christ, of harboring the fugitive antichrist. Mankind tends to accuse others of being what we all at one time are guilty of. The finite natural mind of man is at enmity with the infinite Spirit of God… for it is not subject to the law of God, neither indeed can be" (Rom. 8:7). "For now we see through a glass darkly; but then face to face; now I know in part; but then shall I know, even as also I am known" (I Cor. 13:12). We will know ourselves as the Seed of the reflection of the living God.

When we individually overcome the antichrist on a personal level in the spirit realm, it will be reflected on earth, with faith released for the power of God to deal with any possible emergence of an individual or group exhibiting an antichrist spirit of dominance over others, in political or other avenues of power that would bring harm to His creation. "Surely he shall deliver us from the snare of the fowler" (Ps. 91:3).

"*It is* time for *thee* Lord, to work: for they have made void thy law" (Ps. 119:126). We live in a time when the principles of God are treated with contempt by those who know not their maker and redeemer. "Woe unto the world because of offences! For it must needs be that offences come; but woe to that [seed of] man by whom the offence cometh!" (Matt. 18:7). "Woe unto him that striveth with his maker" (Is. 45:9). The Incorruptible Seed within man would never strive with His maker.

"*Was* not Esau, Jacob's brother? saith the Lord: yet I loved Jacob [Lamb] And I hated Esau, [goat] and laid his mountains [Edom] and his heritage waste for the dragons of the wilderness. Whereas Edom [Esau] saith, We are impoverished, but we will return and build the desolate places; thus saith the Lord of hosts, They shall build, but I will throw down; and they shall call them, The border of wickedness, and The people against whom the Lord hath indignation forever" (Mal. 1:2-4). A lake of everlasting fire is prepared for the devil and his angels. These are the vessels of wrath fitted for destruction—the man of sin, who is subject to death—at enmity with God—he is fuel for the consuming fire of God. "And He shall set the sheep on His right hand, [Seed of God] but the goats on the left hand, then shall He say to the goats on His left hand; Depart from me ye cursed, *into everlasting fire prepared for the devil and his angels*" (Matt. 25:33.41).

The truth of the matter is really very simple—we shall *all* dwell in the everlasting fire, in the presence of the Holy Spirit— however, only those who can dwell with everlasting burnings will remain un-singed. "… Who among us shall dwell with the devouring fire? Who among us shall dwell with everlasting burnings? He that walketh righteously and speaketh uprightly, he that despiseth the gain of oppressions, that shaketh his hands from holding of bribes, that stoppeth his ears from hearing of blood, and shutteth his eyes from seeing evil" (Is. 33:14.15).… "when thou walkest through the fire, thou shalt not be burned; neither shall the flame kindle upon thee (Is. 43:2). "… under *His glory* He shall kindle a burning of a fire. And the light of Israel [Holy Spirit] shall be for a fire, and His Holy One for a flame [His Seed in us] and it shall devour His thorns and His briers in one day…And it shall come to pass in that day *that* the remnant of Israel, and such as are escaped of the house of Jacob, shall *no more stay upon him that smote them,* [man of sin] but shall stay upon the Lord, the Holy One of Israel, in truth. The remnant shall return, *even* the remnant of Jacob unto the Mighty God… the consumption [fire] decreed *shall overflow with righteousness.* For the Lord God of hosts shall make a *consumption*; even determined, in the midst of all the land" (Is 10:16.17.20.21).

He knows whom He loves, and He loves whom He knows, in every person. We are so used to the love him—love-him not—approach, that it is easy for us to be blinded to the full meaning of the at**one**ment on the Cross once and for all. Christ died for the ungodly—He died for the souls that are in bondage to the ungodly nature of the man of sin—and now it is time for the ungodly to die for Christ. "For whosoever will save his life shall lose it: and whosoever shall lose his life for my sake shall find it" (Matt. 16:25). This refers to offering up the seed of man that pretends to be us, in exchange for the Seed of God to become us. We can never become God, but He desires to become us, through His Holy Seed. For that purpose we were created—to be the dwelling place for His Spirit.

Summary: The Seed of His Image, nature and character is resident in us all. "… But thou hast made me to serve with thy sins, thou hast wearied me with thine iniquities" (Is. 43:24). *"Behold I am pressed under you, as a cart is pressed that is full of sheaves"* (Amos 2:13). No matter how deeply He is buried within us, His Seed, though dormant still remains—containing life with its full potential of reproducing the Garden of Eden within us. A small acorn can lie dormant until certain conditions are present to bring forth the life that is contained within. This made on earth, visible reality, is a reflection of the invisible creation of the Seed of God in man, revived and our souls reborn, through the shed blood of Jesus and the power of the Holy Spirit. "…that they may be called trees of righteousness, the planting of the Lord, that He might be glorified" (Is. 61: 3).

The trees of righteousness, the planting of the Lord–is the Tree of Life that was breathed into the garden of man's soul at the beginning of creation, when God breathed His

Seed—the breath of His Life into Adam and Adam became a living soul.

Man with his free will and choice—chose to plant another tree in the garden of his soul, the tree of the knowledge of good and evil, a tree that produced the seed of death in him. Of the two trees in the Garden of Eden, man was warned that he would surely die if he partook of the fruit from the forbidden tree. Man reflected the beauty of the garden until he was cast out of the garden into a place that was a reflection of himself; a place bearing not fruit, but thorns and thistles—a picture of the desolation he had produced in his own soul.

References made to the Seed of God being in a state of dormancy, does not mean the dormancy is due to the Seed of God being asleep, it simply means that *our souls are asleep* to the realization of the presence of the Seed of His Image within us. Due to the limitations God placed on Himself, He remains inactive until called upon by being acknowledged and accepted. Some enter the Kingdom drawn by love, others enter in by fear, but we *all* enter by grace and mercy through the shed blood of Jesus Christ. God's grace becomes God's mercy at work in us: by His grace we are saved. "It is of the Lord's mercies we are not consumed, because His compassions fail not" (Lam. 3:22). He has made preparation for us to dwell in the presence of the Holy Spirit through the baptism of fire. We are tried in the fire that consumes all that offends. "But He knoweth the way that I take when He hath tried me I shall come forth as gold" (Job 23:10).

"He shall call upon me and I will answer him" (Ps. 91:15). His ear is always open to those who call out to Him. "For it is written, as I live saith the Lord, every knee shall bow to me, and every tongue shall confess to God" (Rom. 13:11). His ear is ever open to hear and answer the cry of His Seed in *every* soul.

Our bodies become the crucible (definition: earthen pot—container that can withstand high heat—a severe test or trial), where the tares and chaff are consumed, like Shadrach, Meshach and Abednego "...upon whose bodies the fire had no power, nor was an hair of their head singed, neither were their coats changed, nor the smell of fire had passed on them" [we, His Seed, also remain un-singed] (Dan. 3:27).

Thank you Lord for being more,
Than all my heart was hoping for.
Thank you for a love toward man,
More precious than he could understand.

Forgive me Lord, I never knew,
What loveliness I'd find in you.
For never trusting you could see
Your Holy Seed pressed down in me.

Thank you Lord, you never paused,
For wickedness, but knew the cause.
And thank you Lord, your love has spared
The soul of man, because you cared.

Chapter Nine

Rightly Dividing the Word of Truth

"And then will I profess unto them, I never knew you: depart from me, ye that work iniquity" (Matt. 7:23). He is speaking of the strange plant that was sown in His garden after He gave the man Adam dominion over His creation. "Yet I had planted thee *a noble vine, wholly a right Seed;* how then art thou turned into the degenerate plant of a strange vine unto me?" (Jer. 2:21). Jesus, speaking to His disciples said: "Every plant, which my heavenly Father hath not planted, shall be rooted up" (Matt. 15:13).

The concept of judgment is so prevalent among us it is difficult for us to refrain from condemning the whole man. "For the Word of God is quick and powerful, and sharper than any two-edged sword, piercing even to the dividing asunder of soul and spirit, and of the joints and the marrow, and is a discerner of the thoughts and intents of the heart" (Heb. 4:12). This is a reference to dividing the soul from the seed of disobedience—clearing the way for a more perfect union between the soul and the Spirit of God. Jesus spoke these words: "Suppose ye that I am come to give peace on earth? I tell you nay: but rather *division*" (Luke 12:51). "Think not that I am come to send peace on earth: I came *not* to send peace but a *sword*" (Matt. 10:34).

Only God can make the division between who we really are and the counterfeit we have believed ourselves to be. "For the Lord looketh on the heart" (I Sam. 16:17). He is able to rightly divide our true identity from the imposter. He and He alone knows where to wield the two-edged sword to make the precision cut between our soul and the spirit that usurped our identity—the parasite attached to the chaff on our soul.

Mistletoe on a tree is a perfect example: because it is a parasite attached to the tree, and looks to be a part of the tree, when its very existence is sustained by draining the life from the tree. This same process is at work in man, resulting in aging and eventually death. Death being—*the last enemy*—**to be overcome.** "The last enemy that *shall be* destroyed is death" (Rev. 15:26).

The Inheritance

The only war necessary to be waged, is for every man to allow the Spirit of the Living God to divide and conquer within him. This warfare is not from man to man, but from seed to seed. Our souls get caught in the middle of the conflict that is characteristic of the duality in the nature of the natural man. We need to fully occupy our own land (body), rather than trying to exercise dominion over someone else. The greater and most important meaning of the land we are to inherit is the land *in* which we live, however, the insatiable nature of the enemy of our souls tries to usurp not only our souls, but also everything that belongs to us, both naturally and spiritually. When we have conquered and taken possession of our own personal territory within—by yielding to the Holy Spirit—then and only then will we truly have victory both within and without.

"Ask of me and I shall give thee the heathen for thine inheritance and the uttermost parts of the earth for thy possession" (Ps. 2:8). This has a two-fold meaning, the literal land that is historically referred to, and the spiritual significance in reference to taking back into our possession what was usurped from the beginning of creation. It does not mean that we are to continue fighting among ourselves against those who are foreign to us, but within ourselves, through the power of the Holy Spirit—to take the whole land from the imposter—the parasite that claims to be a part of our tree, while its survival is being sustained by draining our life's energy.

All wars within and without are rooted in the tree of the knowledge of good and evil. There is no such thing as a holy war—there is nothing holy about the death and destruction of war. This side of the Cross, can be compared to Jesus asking His disciples to cast their nets on the other side of the boat, and the nets could not bear the weight of all the fish. This is a *type* of being on this side of the Cross, where all are gathered in, and the separation of the good fish from the bad is done in each one of us individually.

We are living in the time of famine for the Word of God. "Behold, the days come saith the Lord God, that I will send a famine in the land, not a famine of bread, nor a thirst for water, but of hearing the words of the Lord" (Amos 8:11).

In the same manner Joseph's actions prepared for the famine in Egypt; Jesus's sacrifice on the Cross prepared the way for us to receive life through redemption, to supply all we need. The storehouse within us is full; for all that we have need of is contained within the Holy Seed. The Holy Spirit holds the key to the storehouse and our soul holds the lock which is our freewill and choice. We must allow the Holy Spirit to unlock and open the prison doors that have held us captive and receive the life provided for us through the Cross. When we yield ourselves to the Holy Spirit, the storehouse can release all that is needed to revive and deliver us from the famine of the soul, by the unveiling of the Word of Truth contained in the Holy Seed. "And they shall teach no more every man his neighbor, and every man his brother, saying Know the Lord: for they shall all know me, from the least of them unto the greatest of them, saith the Lord" (Jer.31:34). Through the Seed of the Image of God—in the secret place of the Most High, where we abide under the shadow of the Almighty, we contain all of the truth and understanding that we have need of.

"In the beginning was the Word, and the Word was with God, and the Word was God" (John 1:1). His Seed was created in His Image by His spoken Word; His Word is His Life, and we are *all* His heirs. The Word has been made available to us through the ages, but instead of an equal understanding and sharing; it has been misunderstood by many and scorned by others—divided by man into various denominations, like the dividing of His garments among the soldiers at His crucifixion—each one judging his neighbor, instead of rightly dividing the Word of God, so that it can rightly divide our true identity from the imposter. "Incline your ear, and come unto me: hear, and your soul shall live. Seek the Lord while He may be found call upon Him while He is near" (Is. 55:3-6).

Not to the boots, who with hacksaws and shovels
Storm through the Word and dissect God at will,
Comes the unveiling of Christ and His purpose
That which is hidden, remains hidden still.

But to the small feet of innocent longing,
Unto the seeker of God, not His power,
Comes revelation of Him who has loved us
Raindrop by raindrop and flower by flower.

When the Word of Truth is rightly divided—it becomes *for all*—instead of a judgment against all or, for some—and against some. There may be many paths that lead us *to the path of God,* but they must all converge on the **one** and **only path to God,** for: "Wide *is* the gate, and broad *is* the way [of the natural man] that leadeth to destruction… straight is the gate and narrow *is* the way [of the Seed of God] which leadeth unto life" (Matt: 7:13.14). The many paths *that lead us to* **the** *path of God,* are like individual bodies of water—fighting their way through rocks and debris—rushing onward through rivers to reach the sea, to be united and blended into one body. It can be compared to the journey of our individual souls—rushing through different paths in the river of life, to reach the Son, to be reconciled to the Father—fitly joined into one body—the body of Christ—who is our head. "So we being *many* are *one* body in Christ and everyone members of another" (Rom. 12:5).

Reflecting His Image and His Likeness

As Jacob supplanted Esau, so are we, through Christ to supplant and *overcome* the man of sin. "To him that *overcometh*, will I grant to sit with me in my Fathers throne, *even as I also overcame,* and am set down with my Father in His throne" (Rev. 3:21). Christ came to redeem our souls from our false identity, replacing it with His likeness, demonstrating by His very nature—His identity as our own. His appearance on earth was like a **mirror**—reflecting His Image back to us, revealing our true identity—an identity *heretofore* unknown to man—a revelation of who we are as well as the revelation of who He is…"When He shall appear we shall be like Him; for we shall see Him as He is" (I John 3:2). We shall see Him as the **mirror** of our true identity; then we, like Jacob will see God face to face—***His face reflecting in our own.***

> Open, Lord my eyes to see
> The fervent hope you have in me.
> For I was formed to mirror you,
> And what you've planned, you well can do.
>
> Take, dear Lord my merest songs,
> For unto you they all belong,
> And out from you they ever flow,
> And unto you they each shall go.
>
> Give me life producing words,
> Gentle heart songs that when heard
> Bring your peace like Noah's dove,
> Created to express your love.

When righteousness with healing wings
Reveals the utter truth of things
And souls at last shall understand,
The mystery of life—Christ in man.

We have been given the freedom to choose whom we will serve, just as Adam and Eve made their choice. **We are no longer bound by their choice—only our own.** Those who desire the flesh are permitted to serve the insatiable, demanding flesh nature, constantly wanting and demanding more, yet never appeased. We are allowed the freedom of choice to choose against our own souls if we desire to follow the same course of action as Adam and Eve. With so much dross and so little gold—the purifying flames of love must increase.

While the Spirit of Life in Christ Jesus, that makes us free from the law of sin and death, is waiting in the wings, the players on the stage of the world continue to struggle with good and evil to no avail—a battle that has never been, nor ever can be won by man. As wars and rumors of war continue to rage, the Spirit of Truth and Life await until mankind recognizes the futility of his own efforts, and *awakens* to acknowledge and submit to the Incorruptible Seed of God within him.

The 36th chapter of Ezekiel has twenty-four references to what the Lord will do for us and what He will cause to happen for us. Verse 37 sums up the whole chapter. "Thus saith the Lord God; I will **yet** for this be inquired of by the house of Israel **to do it for them**" (Ez. 36: 37). We are to cease from our own self efforts and covenant with Him to do it for us—providing the faith and trust necessary for Him to do it.

Jesus walked the earth as a man, revealing the nature and character of God that was resident in Him. "And I fell at His feet to worship Him, and He said unto me, See *thou do it* not: I am thy fellow servant, and of thy brethren that have the testimony of Jesus: **Worship God; for the testimony of Jesus is the spirit of prophecy**" (Rev: 19:10). Worshiping God is not *only* for the sake of honoring His Sovereignty, but for our sakes, to lead us beyond ourselves and to prevent us from focusing on the fruit of the tree of the knowledge of good and evil—that produces the conflicting duality of either self-exaltation or self-intimidation. Jesus came in the spirit of prophecy, to testify by example to the truth of our original, nature—the **Express Image of God.**

Another aspect of this scripture worth pondering: The Old Testament is the spirit of prophecy, testifying of Jesus, fulfilled in the New Testament, revealing grace. The testimony of Jesus in the New Testament, also referred to as the spirit of prophecy, testifies of the Holy Spirit, revealing mercy. The Comforter that Jesus sent was to fulfill the prophecy of completing the work of the Holy Spirit in man, to reproduce the Image of God, by bringing resurrection life back into the Seed of Gods own planting within man.

Every aspect of Jesus's life can be seen as descriptive of the work of the Holy Spirit within man—from the stable to the Cross and from the grave to His glorious resurrection. We as the children of God are to be Living Testaments through the Holy Spirit—all that remains is for the plan of the ages to be manifested in man. Truly, this is the day that the Lord has made and we are privileged to be the generation that will witness the Kingdom of God coming in great power and great glory.

Jesus *is* the *living revelation* of the nature, character and Image of God that was resident in Him—so we could see and understand the potential for the same within us—is our right—our true inheritance. Sin reigned under the law that man could neither keep nor fulfill. Jesus came to do what man could not. Only the one who gave the law could fulfill it, so He—through His Father—fulfilled all the law so that it could be done away with, and be replaced by the greater: "The Spirit of Life in Christ Jesus that makes us free from the law of sin and death" (Rom. 8:2). The law served its purpose, but it is impossible for unregenerate man to keep the whole law—making it of none effect. "Knowing this, *that the law is not made for a righteous man,* but for the lawless and disobedient, for the ungodly and for sinners, for unholy and profane..." (I Tim: 1:9). "He that is unjust, let him; be unjust still: and he which is filthy, let him be filthy still: and he that is righteous, let him be righteous still: and he that is holy let him be holy still" (Rev. 22:11). The Incorruptible Seed remains true to His nature of righteousness and holiness—while the seed that causes man to sin remains true to its unjust nature.

Jesus, the only begotten Son of God—born of a virgin—through an Immaculate Conception, by the Holy Spirit, made it possible for us to be born again through the same process of being conceived immaculately by the Holy Spirit. He came as the Seed of God matured to its full potential, to show us our true identity, containing the same potential for maturity as rightful heirs of God. By His Grace we are saved—through His Mercy we will be restored to our original design and purpose. Our souls united as one with the Father and Son—through the

Holy Spirit—will soon *behold* the Kingdom of our God coming in *great power* and *great glory.*

Summary: He took the sin nature upon Himself, though He knew no sin. He took on the identity of man, so that man could be free from the stain of original sin and its consequences. "Christ hath redeemed us from the curse of the law, being made a curse for us" (Gal. 3:13). The resulting curses that were the consequences of sin are found in Deuteronomy the 28th chapter. It shows what a wondrous redemption is ours through Jesus Christ and reveals numerous curses and plagues without number—to sum it all up the 61st verse tells us that every sickness and every plague, which is not written in this book of the law is included in the curse that we are redeemed from. We must know the truth before we can be made free. Let us not perish as people without a vision—for a lack of knowledge and understanding of the truth.

The choice remains with us, He does not force His will upon us, but says: "Behold, I stand at the door, and knock: if any man hear my voice, and open the door, I will come in to him and will sup with him, and he with me" (Rev. 3:20). "**A**sk and it shall be given unto you; **s**eek, and ye shall find; **k**nock, and it shall be opened unto you. For every one that asketh, receiveth; and he that seeketh, findeth; and to him that knocketh, it shall be opened" (Matt. 7:7.8). Don't expect God to break down the door and enter where He has not been invited. Only the man of sin operates by using force, against our will. Any time we feel compelled or pushed to act in ways that are against sound reasoning, we should wait and seek guidance before action. God's tugs and nudges are gentle and not forceful, He never pulls or pushes, but is a gentle Shepherd who lovingly leads His sheep—those who by *choice* are willing to follow and be *guided* by Him.

Ask

Seek

Knock

The choice of action is ours—He knocks—*we* open—*we* knock—He opens; or *we may choose against our own souls* and ignore His loving sacrifice that enables God to deliver us from the kingdom of darkness into the Kingdom of His dear Son. *How can we neglect so great a salvation?*

Conclusion

"God has dealt to every man the measure of faith" (Rom. 12:3). What we believe depends on where our measure of faith is applied, whether it is placed in truth that produces life, or in deception that produces death. Mankind has a tendency to blend various shades of gray from good and evil. "For all the promises of God in Him *are* yea, and in Him Amen, unto the glory of God by us" (II Cor. 1:20). No matter how well we blend the shades of gray in our attempt to balance the good and evil in our lives, the fruit of that tree remains the same.

It is the nature of the natural man to attempt to blend black and white—creating the gray zones of compromise to blind us to the reality of our need to be transformed—under the guise of "We are good people—we don't do bad things." Thank God, there is a good side of the tree, even though it is better to choose the good and abhor evil—if we could redeem ourselves by being good, why would Jesus have willingly given Himself into the hands of man, to suffer such a cruel death to redeem us? Remember the forbidden tree is the tree of the knowledge of *good* and evil—the wrong tree producing the wrong seed— bearing the fruit of death. "But we are all as an unclean *thing*, and all **our** righteousness's *are* filthy rags; and we all do fade as a leaf; and our iniquities, like the wind, have taken us away" (Is. 64:6). Our iniquities have taken us away from the truth and reality of our being, holding us captive through our lack of understanding.

His Seed within us does not, will not and cannot sin. It is still a matter of *choosing* life or death as it was in the beginning of creation. "I have set before you, life and death, blessing and cursing: therefore *choose* life that both thou and thy Seed may live" (Deut. 30:19). Since Christ has redeemed us from the curse of the law, we are no longer subject to the curse it is up to us with the freewill and *choice* we have been given, to *choose* life and live.

Our soul is the vehicle through which faith operates, whether for us or against us. Misdirected faith has power over us as well as positive faith, resulting in the fruit of righteousness or unrighteousness. Conforming is when we allow ourselves to be subjected to outside influences—transforming is when we are changed from the inside out—rather than allowing the outside in. "And be not conformed to this world: but be ye transformed by the renewing of your mind, that ye may prove what *is* that good and acceptable, and perfect will of God" (Rom. 12:2).

The soul, through the grace of God, by His Seed that dwells in us, through the power of the Holy Spirit is united to Christ as His Bride. The natural man is subject to the seed of evildoers that deceives our soul, trying to blind us to our rightful inheritance—redemption through the grace of Jesus Christ—bought and paid for in full at Calvary.

God did not create us *just* so He could have company to fellowship with. God created man in His own Image, both male and female for a specific purpose, separating the female from the male via the rib; we were created to be the Express Image of God. "A body thou hast prepared for me" (Heb. 10:5). "I beseech you therefore brethren by the mercies of God that ye present your bodies a living sacrifice, holy and acceptable unto God, which is your *reasonable service*" (Rom. 12:1). How can it possibly be an unreasonable request, when it is the whole purpose for our existence from the beginning?

In the beginning: God formed the woman from the man. Her interference resulted in God allowing her to experience the travail of the natural birth process by man being formed in the woman. "A woman shall compass a man" (Jer. 31:22). Through the overshadowing of the Holy Ghost, by an Immaculate Conception; God's only begotten Son was placed in the womb of a virgin to be born through the natural birth process as the Son of Man—containing the Seed of the Image of God. Creating a new man—a new creation—revealing our true nature created in God's Image. A Seed that had long been buried and forgotten by man, until Jesus Christ came in the Image of that long lost child in each one of us to unite our souls to our true parentage. He came to revive the Seed of His Image that has been buried beneath the iniquity in man unable to rise. "Behold I am pressed under you as a cart is pressed *that is* full of sheaves" (Amos 2:13).

"And all things are of God, who hath reconciled us to himself by Jesus Christ… To wit that God was in Christ reconciling the world unto himself, **_not imputing their trespasses unto them…_**" (II Cor. 5:18.19). It is the deceiver and the accuser of the brethren that imputes **his** trespasses to **us,** and leaves the soul to bear the guilt and consequences of the deeds perpetrated by the man of sin, who says: "we have made lies our refuge and under falsehood have we hid ourselves" [leaving the soul to bear *all* of the blame for the deeds done in the body] (Is. 28:15). The true nature and character of God has been distorted by the deceiver since the beginning of time, when man was tempted to question God's intentions; the soul's concept of God is still being distorted by the same deceiver—and God's intentions are still being questioned. "Hath God said?" (Gen. 3:1).

Jesus did not fail: He fulfilled all that was in the purpose of God for Him to accomplish. He overcame all that has overcome us, through our lack of vision concerning our position and standing in Him—due to our lack of knowledge and understanding. By His stripes we were healed from every sickness and dis-ease, and of sin and its wages, which is death.

When Jesus spoke these words: "… I am not sent but unto the lost sheep of the house of Israel" (Matt. 15:24), He was referring to the Seed of God—His lost sheep, hidden in man. "My sheep wandered through all the mountains, and upon every high hill: yea, my flock was scattered upon all the face of the earth, and none did search my sheep, and seek them out. And I *will bring them out from the people*, and gather them from the countries, and will bring them to their own land, and feed them… I will seek that which was lost, and bring again that which was driven away, and will bind up that which was broken, and will strengthen that which was sick…" (Ezek. 34: 6.11.13.16).

We are born on earth as the seed of man, in need of redemption. Without the shedding of blood there is no remission of sin. Jesus was not just a good man and a prophet—without the shedding of His blood, as a willing offering, the Seed of God within our earthen vessels would *forever* remain dormant. Only the sinless blood of Jesus can revive the Seed of God in man. It parallels our blood types—that limit us to only being transfused with the same blood type. The sinless Seed of God can only be revived by sinless blood—only Jesus carried the blood type to revive God's Seed in us.

He is the door into the sheepfold, where the Seed of the Image of God resides in man. "Verily, verily, I say unto you, he that entereth not by the door into the sheepfold, but climbeth up another way, the same is a thief and a robber...this parable spake Jesus unto them: but they understood not what things they were...verily, verily, I am the door of the sheep...I am the door: by me if any man enter in he shall be saved...I am come that they may have life and have it more abundantly...I am the good shepherd: the good shepherd giveth His life for the sheep. I am the good shepherd, and know my sheep, and am known of mine." (John 10:1.6.7.9.10.11.14).

Man may attempt to enter into the sheepfold by climbing in another way—through various forms of religion, man may *imitate* righteousness, however, all must enter in through Jesus Christ—the true Shepherd of the sheep. Only the sinless blood of Jesus can atone for the shedding of the sinless blood of Abel, *who represents the Seed* of *the Lamb,* that was slain at the foundation of the world, *within* Adam and Eve—their choice put to death their identity—the Lamb that was the source of life within them. They exchanged their life—for the law of sin and death. Through Jesus Christ we are able (Abel) to have an exchanged life—exchanging the law of sin and death for our true identity: "For the law of the Spirit of life in Christ Jesus that makes [us] free from the law of sin and death" (Rom. 8:2).

For Jesus to legally be on earth He had to be born to a natural woman through a natural lineage, God met all of the legal requirements of finding *faith* in chosen men and women, to prepare the way for His coming. His lineage being the tribe of Judah necessitated His coming to the Jews, being born in Bethlehem of Judea. "He came unto His own and His own received Him not" (John 1:11).

A division created by civil strife divided the children of Israel into two tribes; the northern tribe of the House of Israel, made up of ten tribes, and the southern two tribes, called the House of Judah. The northern tribes were carried away into captivity by the Assyrians—where they were later dispersed—causing them to be referred to as the ten lost tribes. One hundred and thirty years later the southern tribe was taken captive by the Babylonians, with a remnant returning to Palestine after seventy years in captivity—placing the tribe of Judah in the area where Jesus was born. His reference to being, sent to the *lost sheep* of the House of Israel had a natural and a Spiritual significance. His natural legal right to being on earth was through the natural lineage of Abraham, Isaac and Jacob—His Spiritual *mission* on earth was—coming to be received, by the sheep who *do hear* the voice of the Shepherd and will *follow no other*—and for the redemption of souls, to revive The Seed of the Image of God, hidden in everyman—His lost sheep—the Seed of His Image. "He calleth His own sheep by name, and leadeth them out. And when He putteth forth His own sheep, [Seed] He goeth before them, and the sheep follow Him: for they know His voice. And a stranger will they not follow, but will flee from Him: for they know not the voice of strangers" (John 10:3-5).

One of the purposes of this book is to reveal the identity of the lost sheep of Israel hidden in every man. *A people—within a people.* It is time for the ingathering of the sheep and the separation from the goats, as chaff is separated from wheat. It is past time for us to awaken. "Awake thou that sleepest and arise from the dead and Christ shall give thee light" (Eph. 5:4). We must not allow blindness to the truth, to continue to rob us of what He has accomplished through His sacrifice. *He did not die in vain—when He said it is finished—it was done!* Our *response* to His *ability* (responsibility) is simply to believe, receive and live the life He has provided. The main focus of the enemy of our souls, is to intercept and prevent man from comprehending and experiencing the finished work of the Cross, by blinding us to the truth.

The good side of the tree of the knowledge of good and evil can imitate righteousness, but it can only produce a religious spirit that operates under the law of sin and death to no avail. God's greatest gift to man is His only begotten Son—His grace to us through Jesus Christ our Lord—even the forgiveness of sin. God's greatest treasure is His Seed in man. "... *let them hear, and say, it is truth*" (Is. 43:9).

Three men dying on a hill:
Two are thieves—the third is killed
Daring to expose man's will.
The melancholy crowd is still.
On the left their hangs a thief.
His name is Flesh—He's void of grief,
Concerning any crime—relief
Is all he values, all he seeks.

On the right, confused and dazed.
Hangs a thief named Soul—His gaze
Is backward to his clever ways
Which brought him to this day of days.
In their midst the Spirit rests
His battered chin upon His chest,
Resolutely He's acquiesced
To suffering: Divine request.

The one named Flesh then calls aloud,
Mocks the Spirit to the crowd,
"If you're the Christ," he cries, unbowed
"Save yourself and us," he howls
The Spirit stoops to no replies,
Answering no jerring cries
As Flesh is growing to despise
The Light that flickers in His eyes.

The Soul now lifts his voice at last,
A little of his fog has passed.
Indignation now has cast
Aside despair—He speaks aghast.
"Do you have no fear of God?
You and I deserve this rod,
But He in innocence has trod.
Perhaps, He truly is the Son of God."

He turns his head—the Spirit nods.
"Remember me, Lord when you come
Into your Kingdom," then the hum
Of noises, voices coming from
The crowd below—are silenced—as,
Alive with Love while yet He dies,
"Today," says He—to the Soul—He cries,
"You will be with me in Paradise."

Part II

This portion of the book is for those who hunger and thirst after righteousness. "As the hart [deer] panteth after the water brooks, so panteth my soul after thee, O God. My soul thirsteth for God, for the living God" (Ps. 42:1.2).

Draw Me On

As a deer longs for water,
Thirst I for you.
Draw me on gently,
Lord unto you.

Leave me not pastured,
In grass no more green;
Leave me not thirsty
Along the dry streams;

Feed me, refresh me,
Touch me each morn.
Draw me on gently,
Lord draw me on.

If you can identify with the message in
the above scripture and poem

Part II is for you.

As the spring comes to the garden,
  As its warmth restores the soul,
And the life that has lain dormant
  Wakes! God's promise to behold,
Past the loneliness of winter
  And the snows that hearts can feel
Comes the melting of our sorrows
  In the sunlight that reveals:
Perfect love that has been hidden
  Until the fullness of time,
While the pruning of the branches
  Makes a way for love to shine
While in silence and in longing
  Buds the Seed the Father sows
With the warmth of His own presence
  Bringing forth the perfect rose.

Chapter Ten

Proof of Purchase

When Jesus willingly offered Himself to purchase our salvation; our souls were stamped with His proof of purchase—like having a personal bar code, imprinted within the Seed of His Image, that includes all of His provisions—activated through redemption by the shedding of His blood, reconciling us to God and restoring us to our rightful inheritance as children of God. There is much contained in this imprint, yet to be decoded. His Image is the only true *image*; all others created by the *imagi*-nation of man are false and cannot be compared to the original heavenly design of man created in the Image of God.

God through Jesus—Jesus through the Holy Spirit, and the Holy Spirit through our power of choice, has **empowered us** to take back the birthright and blessing that is our rightful inheritance. Through the power of the Cross, Jesus has made provision for us to reclaim what He purchased with the price of His shed blood. God, not being a usurper, to take back what He has freely given, equipped us through the power of the Holy Spirit to reclaim what was stolen from us through subtlety and deceit.

In the book of Esther, King Ahasuerus gave wicked Haman his ring, seal and authority to do with the Jews as it seemed good to him. Despising the Jews, Haman had letters sent to all the provinces to destroy, to kill and to cause to perish all Jews, young and old. Queen Esther revealed to the king the plot to destroy her people, which would have included her. ... "for the writing which is written in the king's name, and sealed with the king's ring, may no man reverse" (Esther 8:8). The king sent for the scribes and Mordecai dictated a new letter, "Wherein, the king granted the Jews, which were in every city to gather themselves together, and to *stand* for their life, to destroy, to slay, and cause to perish all the power of the people and province that would assault them"... (Esther 8:11).

The condemnation of sin came upon us all when man chose against God. The word picture in the book of Esther reveals that once the decree has gone out, only another decree can nullify the first. Man's sin sent out a decree of condemnation into all the earth, until God sent His Son in the form of man to nullify the first decree. To take away the first required action on their part: they were required to follow the directives of the second decree. Man can still choose to live under the law of sin and death, by ignoring the second decree, that would make him free from the law of sin and death.

Hitler put Haman's decree into action thousands of years after the first decree was sent, committing unbelievable atrocities against humanity in the process. It would be wise for the present day Jewish people to pay heed to their past, recognizing the implications for their future as well. The pattern for their troubles is spelled out in the book of Esther—*when the decree for their destruction was given*. Only by following the directives of the second decree—giving them the authority by order of the King to protect themselves, was the original curse nullified.

There are those who would drive them into the sea—as Pharaoh tried to do, even though he preferred to continue oppressing and enslaving them—until Moses led them out of Egypt, where he pursued them intending to drive then into the red sea—until God parted the waters for them to walk across on dry land. There are those who would totally annihilate them from the earth by exhibiting the nature of the man of sin who opposes the Seed of God that resides in us *all—who unknowingly oppose their own souls,* because the Jews *in type* represent the Chosen Seed of God in every man—putting us *all* on common ground from the alpha to the omega.

The children of Israel, as recipients of the promise God made to Abraham, through Isaac—to be manifested in Jacob, who was renamed Israel—is the visible manifestation of an inward reality. The Nation of Israel, presently occupying only a small portion of the land God appointed to them—parallels and reflects the Chosen Seed within each of us, being restricted to occupying a small portion of the land (body) that God appointed to man in the beginning of creation—this is the true message to be gleaned from the field of His Word, that affects us all. In the beginning what began **in** man—must end **in** man. The earth became and has always been a *reflection*, that continues to mirror the state of being **within** mankind. The conflict and confusion in this world is a reflection of its inhabitants. We must be changed from the inside out to change the conditions in our environment. As it was in the beginning, so it now is: the things we see, being made of things we cannot see—reflecting the unseen by the seen.

"Christ hath redeemed us from the curse of the law [this can also be inclusive of the laws of ancient kings] being made a curse for us" (Gal. 3: 13). The second decree was necessary to nullify the curse in the first decree—requiring the cooperation of the Jews. We have *all* been given the same authority, by putting on the full armor of God, to protect ourselves by embracing the second decree, which was purchased by Jesus's shed blood on the Cross. "Wherefore take unto you the whole armor of God, that ye may be able to withstand in the evil day, *and having done all to stand* (Eph. 6:13). By His grace, we are saved from the condemnation of sin; through His grace and mercy we are restored to our original purpose in God's remarkable plan.

When presented with truth that is unfamiliar, or where there is a lack of understanding, it becomes a matter of debate as we pass through confusion to enlightenment. A child, learning to read will be perplexed and confused until the light of understanding begins to dawn. "In measure when it shooteth forth thou wilt debate with it" (Jer. 27:8). Through the ages, man has debated with and resisted new insights and revelations that do not line up with his preconceived concepts. Consider how many centuries have passed since Jesus walked the earth in a physical body—yet we need not look back but a few hundred years to see how slowly we have progressed from violent reactions to manifestations of God, unfamiliar to man—that resulted in the burning of a young, innocent country girl named Joan of Arc, because she heard what they could not.

The gift of the Statue of Liberty to America from France; *was given* to commemorate the 100th anniversary of America's Independence. The Lady who greets those who enter her harbor;

lifting her flaming torch, welcoming those seeking freedom from oppression—represents more than those involved with her creation may have realized. A gift from France that history has failed to properly recognize and record, and give honor to whom honor is due—one that contributed greatly to America's freedom—Joan of Arc—the true and ultimate gift from France to America—our Liberty.

Our remaining freedoms as a nation today can be attributed to what she heard and what she obeyed, in saving France from English rule. Would it have been possible for the colonists to have chased the English off our shores, if England's military forces had not been divided, by being in conflict with France at the same time as well? In addition to that, a Frenchman by the name of Lafayette came to our aid and helped turn the tide in our favor during the Revolutionary War. If Joan of Arc had not saved France from being swallowed up by English rule, we may have been as well. God made preparation well in advance for our victory to become a nation under God: free to worship without persecution. ***His ultimate purpose for this nation and all of His creation will not be prevented.***

Through passivity, we have allowed some of our precious freedoms to be compromised—freedoms that have taken centuries to gain are now being threatened to an unbelievable extreme. How quickly we have digressed from our status as a free nation under God, to becoming a melting pot of confusion, consisting of the diverse opinions of man. O! How we as a people, do limit our God and weary Him with our iniquities. From every quarter the love for truth is exchanged for a preference or tolerance of evil; as the nature of the natural man, prone to error, conflicts with the truth that God so fervently desires to impart.

> Can my mind yet comprehend,
> The strife in man has always been,
> The flesh that vows, but does not pay,
> Against the Spirit, day by day.
>
> Yet there's a sense within my soul,
> That something still has not been told,
> And that which God would draw to Him,
> Is countered, by a tilt toward sin.
>
> Teach me Lord to understand,
> The mystery of life in man.
> Help me Lord to comprehend,
> The hope of glory—not contemptible blend.

"But the natural man receiveth not the things of the Spirit of God; for they are foolishness unto him: neither can he know *them*, because they are spiritually discerned" (I Cor. 2:14).

It has been a long, slow process of 2,000 years, that the seed of man has resisted, debated with and fought against the Holy Spirit for dominion, a resistance that is still being waged all over the world that seems to be increasing in intensity as we near the end of the dominion of the kingdoms of this world.

"… Woe to the inhabiters of the earth… For the devil is come down unto you, having great wrath, because he knoweth that *he hath but a short time*" (Rev. 12:12). "For there are certain men crept in unawares, who were before of old ordained to this condemnation, ungodly men, turning the grace of our

God into lasciviousness, and denying the only Lord God and our Lord Jesus Christ... But these speak evil of those things they know not; but what they know naturally... Woe unto them! For they have gone in the way of Cain and ran greedily after the error of Balaam for reward,... Raging waves of the sea, foaming out their own shame; wandering stars, to whom is reserved the blackness of darkness forever... These are murmurers, complainers, walking after their own lusts; and their mouth speaketh great swelling words, having men's persons in admiration because of advantage.

"But beloved remember the words spoken before of the apostles of our Lord Jesus Christ; how they told you there would be mockers in the last time, who should walk after their own ungodly lusts. These be they who separate themselves, [from God] sensual, having not the spirit. But ye beloved... Keep yourselves in the Love of God, looking for the mercy of our Lord Jesus Christ unto eternal life. And of some have compassion.... And others save with fear pulling them out of the fire. Now unto Him who is able to keep you from falling, and to present you faultless before the presence of His Glory with exceeding joy. To the only wise God our Savior, be *glory* and *majesty, dominion* and *power* both *now and forever*. A-Men" (Jude: 4.10.11.13.16-17.24.25).

God has always had a purpose and a plan for the earth to be inhabited; the kingdom and dominion were given to His Incorruptible Seed—the only source of life in Adam and Eve at the time it was given. In the fullness of time all will be restored to the rightful owner: God's Seed in each one of us, as individual threads being woven together into the tapestry of God's Kingdom. Dominion was restored on the Cross—

objectively: having actual existence and reality. It remains for us to exercise our power of choice, for the reality to become our energy in motion—uniting our souls with the truth and reality of the Cross.

It is His pleasure to give us the Kingdom—He placed man on earth and breathed the Seed of the Kingdom into him, making him a living soul, placing him in a beautiful garden that was a reflection of his beauty within. "Fear not little flock; for it is your Father's good pleasure to give you the kingdom" (Luke 12:32).

"Thou art worthy, O Lord, to receive glory and honor and power; for thou hast created all things, and for thy pleasure they are and were created" (Rev. 4:11).

Do we really believe that God would allow an enemy to take permanent possession of any part of His creation? He is not powerless to reclaim it. Having given dominion to man, *He is honoring His Word*, it is not in the nature and character of God to take back what He has freely given. Did you ever consider how simple it would be for Him to gather us all back into Himself at once? "If He set His heart upon man, *if* He gather unto Himself His Spirit and His breath; All flesh shall perish together, and man would turn again unto dust" (Job 34:14.15). This being the case, there must be a reason we are still here and have the will to live imprinted within us; otherwise, God would once again be *all in one* and that would be God defeating His *own* purpose.

God breathed His Seed into the soul of man as the only source of life in the soul, when He created Adam and Eve in His Image, both male and female, placing them in the Garden of Eden—giving them dominion over the earth, land, sea and air. Through deception, they gave away their dominion to what was to become an enemy of opposition to their *own* souls and all of their descendants.

Through the working of the Holy Spirit, Jesus came as the visible Image of His Father. The purpose from the beginning was for the invisible to become visible: the plan for man and woman to become the express image of an invisible God, both male and female has only been fulfilled by one man. Could this be the reason why there is so much confusion in the world today concerning gender: is it the result of a limited understanding on earth concerning the heavenly design and purpose?

"Thy will be done in earth as it is in heaven" indicates that we need to get our thinking straight so that heaven and earth are properly aligned by putting our faith in what is true. Since the invisible things of heaven are clearly seen by things (on earth) that are made—what is missing from this picture, in the reflection between heaven and earth? Look around you—*what are we failing to acknowledge concerning heaven that is seen on earth*? Where does our faith need to be applied to bring heaven and earth together in perfect alignment?

Until the whole truth and nothing but the truth is revealed, we are stuck in a matrix surrounded by deception and confusion. The choice of receiving and embracing the truth yet remains with the freewill and choice of the earth's inhabitants.

Jesus came and walked among us to reveal a part of us that we didn't know existed. He purchased our salvation by putting to death the man we believed ourselves to be, revealing the truth concerning our identity by His example: "when He shall appear, we shall be like Him; for we shall see Him as He is"

(I John 3:2). The presence of the Holy Spirit being introduced at Jesus's baptism resulted in the power to begin His earthly ministry—it also produced a reaction from the kingdom of darkness, as it always has and still does.

"And Jesus being full of the Holy Ghost returned from Jordan and was led by the Spirit into the wilderness, being forty days tempted of the devil... And when the devil had ended all the temptation, he departed from Him for a season" (Luke 4:1.2.13). It was necessary for our sakes that He experience this time in the wilderness, to be tempted, yet without sin—tempted in all points, to understand the temptations we face and overcome them in our behalf; "For whatsoever is born of God [His Holy Seed] overcometh the world: and this is the victory that overcometh the world, *even* our faith. Who is he that overcometh the world, but he that believeth that Jesus is the Son of God?" (I Jn. 5:4.5).

All who acknowledge, seek and receive the Holy Spirit are led into the wilderness of doubt and confusion. It is the same as in the beginning. "Hath God said?" This is so predictable because it is the process the natural mind, at enmity with God, goes through causing the soul to question and doubt the validity of any experience or communication with the Spirit of God. When we overcome our doubts and confusion and embrace the reality of God at work in us, we are confronted with yet another predictable tactic: the temptation to be prideful in our experience with God. A wise friend and mentor, Ione Evans, spoke an important truth: "After we give ourselves to God, we need to give Him that great thing we thought He was going to make out of us."

It is a contest for the place in mind and body that the mortal seed of the natural man, who knows nothing of the things of God, has claimed since the day we were born on the earth. The enemy of our soul will rob us with whatever means it takes, by causing us to have self-doubt concerning our true identity, or if that doesn't work, he tries to produce self-exaltation and pride, using any tactic to create disharmony. In order for there to be the: I will go uppers, there have to be the: you will stay downers. We have had enough of duality! What we need is unity among us.

When and wherever the Holy Spirit is activated on earth, there is power released to be received by those who are receptive. God has limited Himself to the point of needing our agreement in covenant with Him, to accomplish His wonders on earth. There is much opposition by those who do not have eyes to see and ears to hear. The natural man defends and protects the kingdoms of this world, to no avail, from the inevitable Kingdom of our God: for the kingdoms of this world **will** become the Kingdom of our God and His Christ.

Summary: God's self-imposed limitations occurred at the time He gave dominion over all the earth to man. Man proceeded to give away his dominion when he partook of the tree of the knowledge of good and evil, forsaking the Tree of Life. Mankind seems to overlook the truth concerning dominion. Adam and Eve *gave away* their God given dominion, while *retaining their power of choice*. Mankind is always blaming God, even though God is staying behind the line *they* drew in the sand; until He is invited to cross over. Jesus made it *possible* for us to be reconciled to God, but it is up to us to *invite* Him as Savior to be the Lord of our lives, which activates and releases the Seed of His Image to dwell within us, instead of allowing ourselves to be lorded over by the man of sin. There are only two choices. *Our choice* is simple—do we want to be *overcome* and *succumb* to the world, or do we want to be *overcomers*? We **must** *choose* wisely.

Chapter Eleven

God's Family in Heaven and Earth

W e should never accept as truth an unfamiliar concept where there is a lack of understanding, without first searching the scriptures and seeking God for the two or three verifying witnesses in His Word, to separate truth from error. "In the mouth of two or three witnesses shall every word be established" (II Cor. 13:1). We should not be so close-minded that we reject truth that is needed in order for God's purpose and plan to be fulfilled. Jesus's appearance on earth as the Living Truth in the flesh, walking among men, created constant debate, because who He was went way beyond their capacity of understanding.

When the apostles were brought before the council, because they chose to obey God rather than man—Gamaliel, a doctor of the law said in their defense: "Refrain from these men, and let them alone: for if this counsel, or this work be of men, it will come to naught; but if it be of God, ye cannot overthrow it; lest ye be found to fight against God" (Acts 5: 38.39). None of us wants to be in a position to fight against God, because of a lack of understanding. The best approach to possible truth, beyond our understanding, is to search out the matter and seek confirmation from the Holy Spirit who came to guide us into all truth. "Howbeit when He, the Spirit of Truth is come, He will guide you into all truth" (John 16:13).

The Moon Connection

A turbulent time for the whole world occurred during the sixties. What those who were not involved in the rebellion against the status quo could see as trouble makers—God, who looks into the heart and not on the outward appearance, saw a multitude of seekers for truth: souls, aware of their need— seeking more than was available to their finite understanding. This period of soul searching and seeking answers, as well as the prayers of those who were concerned because of all that was taking place on the earth during a confusing time of war and change, resulted in a move of God some of us had the privilege to witness and participate in that occurred during the sixties and seventies, that has continued to this present time; while those who are willing to take up their Cross and follow Him are being processed to reflect the nature, character and Image of God.

This phenomenal move of the Holy Spirit in the earth was a time described in the book of Ezra, as a time for a little reviving in our bondage. "And now for a little space grace hath been *shewed* from the Lord our God, to leave us a **remnant** to escape, and to give us a nail in His Holy Place, that our God may lighten our eyes, and give us a little reviving in our bondage" (Ezra 9:8). This dramatic move of God in our time has resulted in the introduction to the continuing work of the Holy Spirit among those who recognize their need, by receiving and embracing this wonderful gift, sent to us from God through Jesus Christ.

A major event in the sixties that was one of the greatest accomplishments of mankind occurred when man landed, placed his flag and walked on the moon. An amazing feat referred to as a "small step for man and a giant leap for mankind," that was witnessed through every form of media available at the time. A scientific marvel and proof of a tremendous advancement in technology that is truly awesome. The moon landing, confusion, turmoil and soul searching of the sixties, brought about the permission needed, in a greater measure than ever before, for God to equip man through the Holy Spirit to regain his lost dominion in the earth. Man has failed to fully comprehend the facts and implications of giving away his God given dominion to an enemy of both God and man. God works within the confines of His covenants and agreements with man—that is why it is so important for us to understand the heavenly design and the *need* God has for us to *aid Him*, so He can in turn come to our aid.

After man gave God permission to do a greater work in our midst by claiming territory for himself that was not included in the *original covenant* with God; we have seen and will continue to see God move in ways never before seen due to the limitations He placed on Himself in His original covenant with man that are no longer as binding. Man invalidated a portion of the original covenant when he claimed the moon for himself. God does not break His covenants with man. It is man that breaks covenant with God.

There was a spiritual as well as a natural occurrence, when man landed and ***set foot*** and flag on the moon. God gave man dominion over all that was on the earth; the fowl of the air and the fish of the sea, but He *did not* give them dominion over the moon. God will not take back what He has given to man, however, His Word clearly states: Eye for eye, tooth for tooth, hand for hand, foot for foot" (Ex. 21:24). Also ***"Every place*** whereon the soles of ***your feet shall tread shall be yours***" (Deut. 11:24). The great wonder *seen* in heaven in the 12th chapter of Revelation is said to be clothed with the sun with the ***moon under her feet***. In this case paraphrasing is needed: foot for foot: moon for earth and earth for moon. The only solution for this territorial dispute is an equal *sharing*. She shares *her moon* and man shares *his earth. Now we will see what great things God will do.*

A phenomenal outpouring of the Holy Spirit that occurred, after permission was granted through man trespassing where he didn't have dominion, has touched every nation, kindred and tongue. Through television, internet and other modern forms of media, the Word of God has gone out, covering more territory than ever before, giving mankind the ability to make the choice of whom they will serve. We are living in the valley of decision, while *we classify ourselves.* Sad but true, this outpouring of the Holy Spirit, while gathering in the first fruits from among men, has also received opposition and resistance from those who *choose to oppose their own souls* by serving the seed of the nature, and character of the natural man that wars against the Spirit of God.

Due to the limited forms of conveyance at the time, Jesus and His followers didn't cover much territory, however, there has been no greater miracle than the continuity of the Word of God through the Holy Spirit—traversing time for thousands of years. Most of the progress made by man in his quest to cover the earth with far reaching communications has only recently been accomplished in a very short period of time. God's ultimate purpose is for the gospel of Jesus Christ to be preached in *all,* the world. We are living in the fullness of time for the restitution of all things, when man will be restored to God's original design and purpose. We are *now* living in the *only* time possible for the fulfillment of the great commission Jesus gave to His disciples: "And He said unto them, Go ye into **all** *the world,* and preach the gospel to every creature" (Mark 16:15). It is plain to see that never before now has this even been a *remote* possibility. Just one click of a *remote* is all it takes to receive and send information all over the world via satellite.

There was a divine purpose for the God given inspiration that enabled man to stake his claim on the moon. How else could such a feat be accomplished without divinely imparted knowledge for its accomplishment? Since God does not encroach upon man's territory and will not take back what He has given to man—having limited Himself according to man's freewill and choice, He has given gifts of inspiration for beneficial discoveries; for example: God always knew that a certain type of mold would yield penicillin; He has given inspiration for all such great discoveries for man's benefit.

In Defense of God

The deceiver, referred to as the accuser of the brethren, began his deception with an accusation against God, that continues to this present time—blaming God as well as us, for his deeds, through deception. It is time for man to stop believing a lie and break every alliance he has ever made with the deceiver's accusations—against us and against God and the Son He sent to redeem us. We should have compassion toward God, for the way mankind resists His Love—His desire is for us to receive a wonderful gift—*the greatest gift He could possibly give to man*—the sacrifice of His Son who purchased our redemption. We have given God a bad rap, which He doesn't deserve, because we lack understanding concerning the *limitations God placed on Himself*, to only intervene when we ask for His intervention. We have to untie His hands so He can untie ours. He is constantly waiting for us to call out to Him, so He can rescue us.

"And the Lord God said, I have surely seen the affliction of my people which *are* in Egypt, (bondage) and have *heard their cry* by reason of their task masters; for I know their sorrows; And **I am come down to deliver** them out of the hand of the Egyptians, and to bring them up out of that land unto a good land and a large, unto a land flowing with milk and honey... **Now** therefore, behold, **the cry of the children of Israel is come unto me;** and I have also **seen** the oppression wherewith the Egyptians oppress them" (Ex. 3: 7-9). The children of Israel being enslaved by the Egyptians is a *type* and *parable of our souls* in bondage and enslavement to the man of sin.

The children of Israel had been in bondage to the Egyptians for approximately 400 years, but God could not come to their aid until He *heard* their cry. Until their cry intensified enough for Him to hear, He had to witness their affliction and oppression—until they finally cried out with such intensity— that their cry came unto Him, a cry that had to come from the *depth of their soul* and not just the murmuring, complaining cry of their flesh. The volume and intensity of the cry of the inhabitants in the earth today needs to increase to the point that our cry for deliverance from bondage is heard loud and clear from the *depth of our souls.* It was when the cry of their souls came unto Him that He sent Moses to be their deliverer, by coming down in the form of a burning bush to get an agreement and to make a covenant with *Moses that gave Him the permission He needed to intervene.*

When we invite the presence of the Holy Spirit, to dwell in us—we become alive with the Holy fire of God—yet we like the burning bush are not consumed. Only the chaff and the tares produced by the man of sin will be consumed. "*It is of* the Lord's mercies that we are not consumed, because His compassions fail not" (Lam. 3:22). Only the *tares* sown in our field (body) and the *chaff* on our soul—along with all that has been produced by our soul's union with the man of sin, is *doomed to be consumed.*

God revealed Himself to Moses by fire—instructing him not to come too close. "And He said, draw *not* nigh hither: put off thy shoes from off thy feet for the place whereon thou standest *is* holy ground" (Ex. 3:5). This was *a sign of a covenant in Israel:* "Now this is the manner in former time in Israel concerning *redeeming* and concerning *changing* for to *confirm* all things; a man plucked off his shoe, and gave it to his neighbor and this is a testimony in Israel" (Ruth 4:7). Another example of God doing all things decently and in order, making covenants with man, for permission to intervene. In addition to it being holy ground by removing his shoes Moses was also yeilding to the authority of the Spirit of God, signifying a covenant between himself and God.

We should truly be convicted and brought to a place of *repentance* for the many ways we offend our God, and His Son. "Thou hast made me to serve with thy sins; thou hast wearied me with thine iniquities" (Is. 43:24). It is a shame and a disgrace to behold the ways that we have abused our God and the Savior He sent, by blaming Him for the conditions in the world that *man has created* from *the choices he has made* since the beginning of creation—when he engineered an *extreme makeover* of God's creation.

Man has a tendency to receive the acclaim for great discoveries and advancements, while blaming God for all the unpleasant happenings that occur in the world. God is not responsible for errors that are the result of *man's wrong decisions and choices*. The conditions in the world since God gave dominion to man are the result of the decisions and choices of man. **God is not to be blamed for the conditions in the world—man has created for himself.** A *world that doesn't even resemble the one God created.* He has gifted us by imparting the vision and inspiration needed to sustain us, because without a vision, *we the people would surely perish from the earth.*

While man has been occupied with building a space station, outside of his God given dominion—God has been building His Kingdom on earth *without observation.* "And when He was demanded of the Pharisees, when the Kingdom of God should come, He answered them and said: "The Kingdom of God cometh **not with observation:** Neither shall they say, Lo here!

or lo there! For behold, the Kingdom of God is *within you*" [a secret garden hidden within our soul] (Luke 17:20.21).

> As ordained from the beginning of creation,
> We shall soon see the manifestation,
> Of man's, transformation, into God's habitation.
> Declaring the end from the beginning.
>
> From ancient times—a Seed—that knows no ending,
> Lying dormant, no longer—not impeded by dearth,
> His Life is quickened and resurrected in our earth,
> As His Kingdom 'with observation,' is visibly birthed.

The Father, Son and Holy Spirit are one, though with diversities of operation. "Now there *are* diversities of *gifts*, but the **same Spirit** [Holy Spirit]. And there are differences of *administrations*, but the **same Lord** [Jesus Christ]. And there are *diversities of operation*, but it is the **same God** [Father] which *worketh all in all*" (I Cor. 12:4-6). The *gifts* of the Spirit are given by the Holy Spirit. The differences of *administrations* are the Lord's and can only be referring to Jesus Christ. The one who is over the *diversities of operation*, that *worketh all in all* is "the Father of our Lord Jesus Christ, of whom the *whole family* in heaven and earth is named" (Eph. 3: 14). God's plan for man is that we *all* be one in Spirit and in Truth. Jesus the immaculate, sinless one, brought forth by the Spirit of God; reveals to us that upon receiving the Holy Spirit, we too are born again of the same Spirit of God through an Immaculate Conception.

Jesus came as the fulfillment of prophecy: He also came *in* the *Spirit of prophecy* to prepare the way for another. "If ye love me keep, my commandments. And I will pray the Father, and

He shall give you **another** Comforter, that He may abide with you forever; *Even* the Spirit of Truth; whom the world cannot receive, because it seeth Him not, neither knoweth Him: but ye know Him; for He **dwelleth with you,** and **shall be in you"** (John 14:15-17).

When heaven and earth were created and the earth was without form and void and darkness was on the face of the deep; the same Holy Spirit that moved upon the face of the waters is the Holy Spirit that overshadowed the Virgin Mary, bringing life to the Seed of the Image of the Father—placed within her womb, through an Immaculate Conception—recreating a new man to establish a new covenant with God—*for man.* The Kingdom of God on earth as it is in heaven.

When Jesus was baptized by John in the river Jordan, He received back into the earth what had not been available since the fatal choice made by Adam and Eve. "I saw the Spirit descending from heaven like a dove, and it abode upon Him" (John 1:32). The Holy Spirit Jesus received at His baptism, is the same Spirit released when He gave up the ghost at His crucifixion and is the Holy Spirit spoken of by Jesus to His disciples when He said: "Nevertheless, I tell you the truth; **it is expedient for you** that I go away: for if I go not away, the Comforter will not come unto you; but if I depart, I will send Him unto you" (John 16:7).

It was expedient that Jesus go away, to apply the blood on the Mercy Seat, so the Comforter *could* come. He, the corn of wheat was *abiding alone* until the Holy Spirit came as Comforter and *multiplier.* Jesus, submitting to the Cross, offering Himself as the corn of wheat, enabled the Holy Spirit to move within our souls reviving us—by multiplying His selfsame Image—

the Image of God, through an Immaculate Conception. His natural birth on earth is a reflection of our Spiritual birth in the invisible realm of heaven. His birth signifying our rebirth.

The fact that the Holy Spirit is translated from the Greek text as *He* should not be a stumbling block to the truth of the matter. In some languages, certain words have a masculine or feminine gender to distinguish their meaning. There are no such distinctions found in the English language. The Greek word for spirit is *pneuma—a neutral word* that can be translated as *either* male or female.

"For **the invisible things of Him** *from the creation of the world are clearly seen, **being understood by the things that are made**, even His eternal power and* **Godhead**; *so that they are* **without excuse**" (Rom. 1:20). When God formed man and breathed His own life into the soul of man, the woman being included in the man reveals the essence of what the *Godhead* consisted of—*unity*—consisting of one Lord, both male and female.

We have *no excuse* for attributing to God an exclusive male identity—when He, Himself refers to His Image as *both* male and female. It could only be possible if the presence of the male species was exclusively on the earth. The presence of the female species on earth overrules that possibility. If it were true, her presence on earth would be completely illegal, *if there was not a pattern in heaven for her to be a reflection of—there could be no her.* If there is no pattern for the female in heaven, then there could be no female on earth. Jesus being birthed by an earthly mother witnesses to the existence of a Heavenly Mother. He could not have one without the other, because the one is a reflection of the other.

The *deflection* of every *reflection* between heaven and earth is the goal of the man of sin, as he tries to block and prevent the Kingdom of God from manifesting in the earth. As long as he can succeed in *deflecting* our Heavenly Mother from the earth—preventing unity between heaven and earth—the full *manifestation* of the Kingdom *cannot* come. This strategy is subtlety calculated to keep the kingdoms of this world from becoming extinct. The man of sin will not willing abdicate, he must be *stripped of his dominion* over man—by *man's choice* of whom he will serve. Man holds *the winning hand,* but until he realizes the *power of his choice,* to *trump* the enemy of our souls, he is *bluffed* into submission through deception. We do not have the power to defeat the man of sin, however, through *our power of choice,* when we accept the redemption, bought and *dearly* paid for through Jesus Christ, and are born anew through an Immaculate Conception by the Holy Spirit—we are *led into the truth*—that makes us free from the law of sin and death. Sin and the wages of sin—which is death—is swallowed up in victory.

Can you picture the men, chosen by King James to translate the Bible from Greek to English, having the choice of either-or-translating a neutral word describing the Holy Spirit into anything *but* He? Another thought to be considered, is that the term man, or man-kind is frequently used to describe the human race as a whole—as the author has done in this book numerous times. Man or man-kind can be *inclusive,* whereas the use of the term woman or woman-kind is *exclusive* and is not used as a description of man or the human race. God who was all in all imparted the Seed of His Image, both male and female, into the man Adam, who became an extension of his Creator. Adam created in the Image of God *containing the woman* was *inclusive*—she was taken from him to be a separate being; *making her exclusive.*

"For this cause, I bow my knees unto the **Father** of our Lord Jesus Christ, of **whom the whole family in heaven and earth is named**" (Eph. 3: 14-15). Every member of the family in heaven and earth is included. The earthly visible things from the creation of the world are an image of the unseen invisible things above.

Families on earth since Adam and Eve at the beginning of creation, have consisted of fathers, mothers and children all sharing a common name, the name of the father of the family—patterned after the *whole* family in heaven.

God, who was complete within Himself, not willing to remain all in one, desiring to be all in all, separating or birthing from himself—created a masculine self and a feminine self to reproduce after their kind, intending to produce a family in their complete image and likeness. It was never Gods intention to be a single parent. He lost the habitation for His Spirit, both male and female when Adam and Eve chose to obey another. When God lost *His place* on earth, they lost the reflection of heaven *on* earth. Abel was the Seed of God, so His Seed could no longer dwell in the flesh on earth, because it was slain in the Spirit realm, the same *had to be reflected on earth.* God lost three Sons who were the Seed of His Image on earth. The Lamb slain within Adam, was an inward reality that was visibly portrayed in Abel, whom Cain slew and Jesus as the only begotten Son of God, a sacrificial Lamb, who took away our sin through redemption, by willingly shedding His blood.

The sorrow experienced by Mary, the mother of Jesus, at the foot of the Cross, is a sorrow that God, as both Mother and Father had to experience as they witnessed the Lamb slain within Adam and Eve, due to their disobedience, that was visibly manifested in Abel and again in Jesus Christ.

God is still desiring to establish His visible Kingdom on earth and be restored to the family that He lost in the beginning—along with the *dividends* that have been *reproduced* from His original investment—which includes all of us—every nation kindred and tongue. It is in this time of the dispensation of the Holy Spirit that we will witness the birth of the new creation in man. Adam and Eve drew a circle around themselves, that excluded their Creator, a pattern man has continued through the ages. Through Jesus Christ—God created a bigger circle—encircling the earth, and including us all.

The Godhead, being referred to as He; when God clearly refers to His Image as both male and female, in Genesis chapter one verse 27—is no more improper than families on earth being called by the father's last name. The Hebrew word for Spirit is Ruah—a feminine word. The Comforter, translated from both Hebrew and Aramaic is a feminine word. In the Greek, since the word for spirit is neutral, it is obvious that the translators using the Greek text *chose* to use the masculine gender when speaking of the Holy Spirit—Comforter—even though *the term Comforter is not usually descriptive of a masculine trait in any language.*

Adam first created and then formed—contained the woman. God took DNA from Adam contained in a rib and formed a vessel to house the identity of the woman. He then allowed them to *classify themselves* and they proceeded to choose a lower road that leads to death rather than the higher form of existence, leading to life. We are also classifying ourselves. There are two roads from which to choose: one to gain and one to lose. We *must* choose wisely.

Ancient, yet youthful, His likeness to see
The Seed of His Image and nature are we.
Marvel of marvels, O! How can it be?
Beauty from ashes—as ashes depart:

His creative genius—A work of art.
Our soul and His Spirit—reunion.
Blending, blending—into a Holy union.
A new beginning in perfect communion.

Summary: We are given the *choice* to *choose* whom we will yield our members as servants to obey. However *comforting* the El Shaddai of God may be to the sheep who hear the voice of the Shepherd, the Holy Spirit is not to be underestimated as protector of what is of God—from what is not. A strong attribute of the Comforter, is the fire of unending love that consumes the dross from the gold, cleansing mankind. The Holy Spirit will make *all* things pure with a cleansing fire—cleansing our souls—by consuming all that offends.

As first-fruits we are given the opportunity to willingly offer up the dross: waste products or impurities—weeds in the garden of our soul—to be consumed, or if we so *choose*, like Thomas, (those who are His at His appearing) we may wait until the fullness of time when all that is offensive to God and cannot stand before the fire of a Holy presence will be consumed by fire; but don't forget, "... but *he himself shall be saved*" (I Cor. 3:13), refers to the place in the soul, where the Seed of God in repose is awaiting deliverance within the vessel that has kept him so restricted and confined—to take His place as the only *energy in motion* in our soul.

We shall surely come forth as gold—tried in the fire of the presence of the Holy Spirit, whether willingly or unwillingly. "*It is of* the Lord's mercies we are not consumed, because His compassions fail not. *They are* new every morning: great is thy faithfulness. The Lord is my portion, saith my soul; therefore will I hope in Him. The Lord *is* good unto them that wait for Him, to the soul *that seeketh* Him. It is good that a man should both hope and quietly wait for the salvation of the Lord" (Lam. 3:22:26).

Chapter Twelve

The Mystery of God

When Joseph dreamed a dream that the sun, moon and eleven stars made obeisance to him, he told his brethren and his father and they rebuked him. His father said to him: "What *is* this dream thou hast dreamed? Shall I [sun] and thy mother [moon] and thy brethren [eleven stars] indeed come to bow down ourselves to thee to the earth?" [Since Jacob, whom God renamed Israel, interpreted Joseph's dream correctly, though questioning its significance—discerning the meaning of the dream he did not dismiss it] "And his brothers envied him; but his father *observed* the saying" (Gen. 37:10.11).

The Holy Spirit was not mentioned in the Old Testament, because the presence of the Holy Spirit had to be withdrawn from the earth when sin entered the world. Scientists say the moon is slowly moving away from the earth and that without the moon, life on earth would change dramatically—it would be devoid of life—since the two are locked together. The farther away the moon, the less stable the earth becomes. The same can be said of the earth being changed drastically and becoming void of life, when the Mother of the Godhead, represented in Joseph's dream by the moon, had to be *put away* from the earth, due to sin in the earth.

A distinctive trait of the Holy Spirit is that of a consuming fire that would consume sin on contact. Adam and Eve would have been consumed along with the sin that was in them. God's Mercy was protecting them by putting their Mother away and placing cherubim with flaming swords to guard the way of the Tree of Life. The Holy Spirit was *put away* from the earth, by the entrance of sin and could not return as the *Life in the Tree of Life*, until the price for atonement was sufficiently paid—not by the High Priests making animal sacrifices once a year, but once and for all by the willing offering of a sinless Lamb without spot or blemish. "Behold the Lamb of God that taketh away the sin of the world. And John bare record, saying, I saw the Spirit descending from heaven like a dove, and it abode upon Him" (John 1:29.30). The only place the Holy Spirit could come to dwell in the flesh, on earth—descending in the likeness of a dove was in Jesus, because He was sinless. *Until He paid the price for the atonement for all sin,* the Mother—Holy Spirit had nowhere else on earth to dwell that was fire-proof.

"Thus saith the Lord, where is the bill of your <u>Mother's</u> divorcement whom I have put away? Or which of my creditors is it to whom I have sold you? Behold, for your iniquities have you sold yourselves, and for your transgressions is your <u>Mother</u> put away" (Is. 50:1). It was a necessary step of faith on the part of the disciples to obey the command to gather together to wait for the Comforter to come when Jesus, "commanded them that they should not depart from Jerusalem, but wait for the promise of the Father, which saith He, ye have heard

of me, but ye shall receive power, after that the Holy Ghost is come upon you: and ye shall be witnesses unto me both in Jerusalem, and in all Judea, and in Samaria, and unto the uttermost part of the earth" (Acts 1:4.8). "And when the day of Pentecost (50 days) was fully come, they were *all with one accord in one place*" (Acts 2:1). Being obedient to Jesus's instructions and being in one accord, to receive the Comforter, was a sufficient agreement on earth, for Her to return. Jesus prepared a welcoming committee to receive Her back into the earth to dwell with mankind—no longer was She *limited* to the one corn of wheat—but was *released* to produce a bountiful harvest in us all.

Jesus ascended to His Father, as the sinless Lamb, willingly slain for the sin of all mankind; as our great High Priest, He entered into the most Holy Place after His resurrection where He offered His shed blood once and *for all* upon the Mercy Seat. When He returned, revealing Himself to His disciples, breathing upon them, He imparted the Holy Spirit to be with them; then He ascended to the *right hand* of His Father so that He could send the Comforter in the Person of the Holy Spirit to *dwell in them*—as the Spirit of Wisdom—imparting understanding to lead them into all truth, and to impart life through an Immaculate Conception.

> Mother of Mercies, Comforter of souls,
> Holy Love—hidden in likeness of a Dove
> Bringing life to your Holy Seed.
> With the fire of Love,
> From your Mercy Seat,

Where the blood of Jesus—willingly shed,
Was offered, in our stead.
Paid in full, He took our place,
Making us one, in your dear Son,
As face to face: we now behold:
His wonderful—Amazing Grace.

Before the Kingdom of God can fully come—removing the prince of this world, the *mystery of God should be finished,* as in the days of the voice of the seventh angel described in the book of Revelation. "But in the days of the voice of **the seventh angel,** when he shall begin to sound, **the mystery of God** *should be finished,* as He hath declared to His servants the prophets" (Rev. 10:7). This end time prophetic scripture indicates that there is an *unfinished mystery* concerning "**even** *His eternal power and Godhead"* (Rom. 1:20).

There must be a sufficient understanding of the truth to produce faith on earth for the kingdoms of this world to become the Kingdom of our God and His Christ. "And the **seventh angel** sounded; and there were great voices in heaven, saying, the kingdoms of this world are become *the kingdom's* of our Lord and of His Christ; and He shall reign for ever and ever" (Rev. 11:15). This scripture declares that the Kingdom comes *after the mystery of God*—concerning the *eternal power and Godhead* is finished in the days of the voice of the seventh angel.

There is a Heavenly Father, a Son and the Holy Spirit: all three are in union as one. The Father and the Son are obviously the pattern for the male species, since Jesus came in a *masculine* form as the Image of His Father. There is only one part of the all *yet* to be properly identified and accepted. We are familiar with the identity of the Father and the Son as the pattern in heaven for the personification of *man* on earth.

Whatever could be the mystery of God on earth, yet to be identified and revealed, who was with God in the beginning, before ever the earth was? Even before they first made in the Spirit and then formed the beginning of their earthly family from the dust of the earth? The one to whom God said: "Let *us* make man in **our image**... in the Image of God created He him; male and female created He them" (Gen. 1:26-27). Created; then formed from the dust of the earth to be the dwelling place on earth for the Father and Mother of all creation: "For the invisible things of Him from the creation of the world are **clearly seen** being **understood** by the things that are **made,** **even** His eternal power and **Godhead.** How much plainer can words describe—mothers on earth as a reflection of a pattern in heaven. Where is the pattern, for the woman separated out of the form of the man Adam, into the form of the one called Eve? Where O where can she be?

The heavenly pattern, for daughters on earth,
Whose new creation, will be brought to birth.
There She is! The New Jerusalem! Mother of us all.
Revealed in the Holy Spirit, to lift us from the fall.

Reunited to Jesus—in the likeness of a Dove,
She appeared as an expression of purest love.
Reuniting the Heavenly Family in the form of man,
Alas, a new beginning—for God's remarkable plan.

There could be no families on earth without mothers. Be reminded once again: "For the ***invisible things*** from creation are ***clearly seen,*** being understood by the things that are made, <u>***even***</u> ***His eternal power and Godhead;*** so that *they* are without excuse" [*they*—means us] (Rom. 1:20). We have no excuse for denying what is clearly spelled out in the Word. This scripture alone is enough to validate the existence of a Heavenly Mother. Eve, a *mother* on earth being *made* in the *form of a woman*, is the witness and evidence of the indisputable fact that the invisible being understood by the things that are made, can only be verifying a *Mother in heaven* as the *pattern* in heaven for Eve, a mother on earth. How can it <u>not</u> be so?

When God took Eve from Adam, she became a visible reflection of the feminine member of the Godhead and was intended to be Her dwelling place, uniting heaven and earth— reaffirming the reality of Her position in the *eternal power and Godhead*—in the reflection between heaven and earth.

There is no better explanation than the obviously *"clearly seen"* identity of the Holy Spirit Comforter. Jesus, after ascending into heaven to sit at the right hand of His Father, sent His Heavenly Mother to comfort His people. Just as His Father finished the work of creation and entered into His rest, Jesus having finished His work on the Cross when He said "It is finished" [entered into His rest seated at the right hand of His Father] (John 19:30). "So then after the Lord had spoken unto them, He was received up into heaven, and sat on the right hand of God" (Mark16:19). "Comfort ye; comfort ye my people, saith your God. Speak ye comfortably to Jerusalem, and cry unto her, that her warfare is accomplished, that her iniquity is pardoned: for she hath received of the Lord's hand double for all *her sins*" (Is. 40: 1.2). "But Jerusalem which is above is free, which is the **mother of us all**" (Gal. 4:26). The natural Jerusalem on earth is a reflection of the Spiritual Jerusalem in the heavens—the *Mother of us all*.

Our freedom is closely tied to our Heavenly Mother, represented by the moon in Joseph's dream in the same way the moon is closely tied to, and affects the stability of the earth. The scriptures clearly state, that their remains a *mystery of God* that will be *unveiled* in the days of the seventh angel.

To be blinded to the existence of such an important person in the Godhead, is not conducive to completion. "Beware lest any man spoil you through philosophy and vain deceit, after the tradition of men, after the rudiments [a field of learning] of the world, and not after Christ. For in Him dwelleth *all* the *fullness* of the *Godhead bodily*, And ye are complete in Him, which *is* the head of all principality and power" (Col. 2:8.9.10).

Who else could the Father have separated out of Himself, but the Holy Spirit, His Image, spoken of as male and female? The only two aspects of Himself mentioned—were reproduced in the form of man—taking the woman out of the man could only be the visible image of what He, Himself consisted of, the invisible—seen by the things that were made. When God said, "Let us make man in our Image, after our likeness..." (Gen. 1:26): He was speaking to the *female counterpart* of Himself.

Jesus's offering on the Cross completely pardoned mankind. A fact that cannot be altered or changed—whether known or unknown—believed or not believed. His mission on earth was to reveal Himself as the *true identity of man;* to willingly shed His righteous blood to take away the sin of the world; enabling Him to introduce His Beloved Mother to mankind, so that we may be rebirthed with the same birth as He, by the moving of the Holy Spirit within our souls, as was done in Mary's womb—bringing new life to the Father's Seed—sown at the beginning of creation. Our rebirth—a reflection of His birth.

Jesus said: "I go to prepare a place for you" (John 14:2). Sending His Mother to comfort us and lead us into all truth was His contribution toward the preparation needed—to prepare us to receive Him upon His returning, to receive us unto Himself. When we see Him we shall be like Him, because as He is, so has *He made preparation for our transformation, to be made like Him in the world.*

Before Jesus gave up the Ghost, on the Cross—one of His last acts was to fulfill on earth what was required before He could send His Heavenly Mother as our Comforter: *He needed a solid agreement from man,* due to the limitation clause in God's original covenant with man. "When Jesus therefore saw His mother, and the disciple standing by, whom He loved, He saith unto His mother, Woman, behold thy son! Then saith He to the disciple, **Behold thy mother!** And from that hour that disciple took her into *his own home*" (John 19:26-28). The parallel between Him asking His disciples to wait in an appointed place for the Comforter to come, by first sending His earthly mother to dwell with the disciple whom He loved, was a solid agreement—a clear reflection between heaven and earth.

Summary: God is operational on earth through covenants and agreements with man, which is somewhat different from man's understanding of being *ruled* by God. The opposite is true: *God limited Himself to man's will and choice, requiring Himself to have man's permission by agreement and covenant to intervene*

—to establish our agreement with His Sovereignty. One of the main purposes for prayer is to declare our devotion—to honor and acknowledge God's Sovereignty—and to petition, seek and invite His intervention. In (Luke 11:1.2), when the disciples asked Jesus how they should pray, His response was a prayer honoring the Father's Sovereignty and an invitation for His intervention, seeking His will and an affirmation of His Kingdom. "And it came to pass, that, as He was praying in a certain place, when He ceased, one of His disciples said unto Him: Lord teach us to pray, as John also taught His disciples. And He said unto them: when ye pray say:

> "Our Father who art in heaven,
> Hallowed be thy name.
> Thy Kingdom come, thy will be done,
> In earth [in us] as it is in heaven.
> Give us this day our daily bread,
> And forgive us our debts,
> As we forgive our debtors.
> And lead us not into temptation,
> But deliver us from evil:
> For thine is the Kingdom,
> And the power and the glory forever.
> A-Men" (Matt.6:9-13).

This prayer has been prayed innumerable times, but how many with devotion and understanding from the heart? What the natural man quotes by rote is not totally lost, but we are told: "What things soever ye **desire**, when ye pray, **believe** that ye receive *them*, and ye shall have *them*" (Mark 11: 24). Those two words, desire and believe, are the difference between a covenant with agreement and mouthing without meaning.

God does everything decently and in order—with man's agreement and cooperation. He does not use force, but *honors His Word* that gave man dominion in the earth. John's action on earth was necessary as an acceptance of Jesus's mother, to be reflected in heaven, preparing the way for the Holy Spirit—Jesus's Heavenly Mother to come to earth as Comforter, to receive and be received. When John was willing to receive Jesus's earthly mother into his own home—he in type—received our Heavenly Mother into the earth as well. Way to go! Thank you! John!

Chapter Thirteen

The Missing Link

The covenant Jesus made with His disciples to wait for the Comforter to come was extremely important—since faith is the necessary element in producing the agreement on earth for God to act. An important mission Jesus had on earth; was to get an agreement from man for the Holy Spirit to be released in the earth. Their faith agreement was verified by their obedience, in waiting at the appointed place for the Comforter to come.

"John answered, saying unto *them* all, I indeed baptize you with water: but one mightier than I cometh, the lachet of whose shoes I am unworthy to unloose: He shall baptize you with the Holy Ghost and with fire" (Luke 3:16). They were baptized with the Holy Ghost and *fire* on the day of Pentecost after the ascension of Jesus into heaven. It is interesting to note the fact that other than the Immaculate Conception of Jesus, the emergence of activity by the Holy Spirit on the world stage—occurred at the time of Jesus's baptism by John in the Jordan River. Throughout the Old Testament, God spoke to man through the Spirit of God, prophets and angels; the terms

Holy Ghost and Holy Spirit are not descriptive of the Spirit of God in the Old Testament.

As previously stated in chapter three, the reason being: the presence of the Holy Spirit had to be withdrawn from the earth due to the sin that had taken up residence in Adam and Eve, because God was protecting them from being consumed along with the sin that was in them. *Until Jesus came*, our Holy Mother and the fire that is a facet of Her presence, had no place on earth to dwell in the flesh, that was fire-proof. An important mission Jesus had on earth was willingly shedding His blood—in offering His blood on the Mercy Seat, He made atonement for the sin in man—making it possible for Her to return to earth.

When man landed and set his feet and flag on the moon, it was on territory that had not been given to him. "Every place whereon the soles of your ***feet shall tread shall be yours***"... (Deut. 11:24). When God spoke those words, first to Moses and then repeated the same to Joshua, He was referring to the earth, which by no means places a limit on the validity of "***Every place.***" The Great Wonder *seen in heaven*: "A woman clothed with the sun and ***the moon under her feet***" (Rev. 12:1), is declaring Her dominion over the moon. God gave man dominion over all that was on the earth, the fowl of the air and the fish of the sea. Since *He did not promise them the moon*, the Spirit of Wisdom can be seen in God's greater purpose for inspiring this accomplishment of mankind—resulting in the Holy Spirit's gaining greater access on earth through a trade agreement, to dwell among men. "Eye for eye, tooth for tooth, hand for hand, ***foot*** for ***foot***" (Ex. 21:24).

"And He showed me a pure river of water of life, clear as crystal, proceeding out of the throne of God and of the lamb, In the midst of the street of it. and on either side of the river, *was there* the tree of life, which bear twelve *manner of fruits, and* yielded Her fruit every month: and the leaves of the tree *were* for the healing of the nations. And there shall be no more curse" (Rev. 22:1.2).

The Tree of Life, seen on both sides of the river is indicative of the reflection between heaven and earth. He is the root and we are the branches; the word for branch is a feminine word, meaning daughters, but does not exclude the sons. God being described as neither-nor, either-or, or both is not limited in distinction and operations by man's classification systems. "There is neither Jew nor Greek, there is neither... male nor female: for ye are *all one* in Christ Jesus. And if ye be Christ's then are ye Abraham's Seed and heirs according to the promise" (Gal. 3:28.29). This doesn't mean that there are not both sons and daughters—the emphasis is not on gender—the emphasis is on the fact that we are *all one in Christ Jesus*—the Seed of the Image of God. One new man—one ancient message—uniting one family in heaven and earth, woven together as one.

"Happy is the man *that* findeth **wisdom** and the man *that* getteth **understanding. She** is more precious than rubies: and all the things thou canst desire, are not to be compared unto **her.** **She is a tree of life** to them that lay hold upon **her:** and happy is *everyone* that retaineth **her.** The Lord by wisdom hath founded the earth; and by understanding hath established the heavens" (Prov. 3:13.15.18.19). By **Wisdom,** refers to the **New Jerusalem Mother of us all**—**founding the earth**—when *understanding established the heavens* and then reflected the same on earth, another example of the reflection between heaven and earth. Wisdom founding the earth—reflects the understanding that has been previously established in heaven.

"Doth not wisdom cry? And *understanding put forth* **her** voice?... Counsel *is* mine, and sound wisdom: *I* **am** *understanding*; *I have strength*... I lead in the way of righteousness, in the midst of the paths of judgment: That I may cause those that love me to inherit substance; and I will fill their treasures. The Lord possessed me in the beginning of His way, before His works of old. I was set up from everlasting, from the beginning, or ever the earth was... When He prepared the heavens, I *was* there: Blessed is the man that *heareth* me, watching daily at my gates, waiting at the posts of my doors. For whoso findeth me findeth *life*, and shall obtain favor of the Lord" (Prov. 8:1.14.20-23.34.35).

Wisdom hath built **her** house, **she** hath hewn out Her seven pillars: [seven Spirits of God?] **She** hath sent forth **her** maidens: [daughters?] **she** crieth upon the highest places of the city, Who so is simple, let him turn in hither; as *for* him that wanteth understanding, **she** saith to him, **Come, eat of my bread, and drink the wine** *which* I have mingled. Forsake the foolish, and live; and go in the way of understanding" (Prov. 9:3-6). This reveals a truth, concerning The Last Supper. When Jesus broke bread and drank wine with His disciples, it was an agreement with a new covenant. "Come, eat of my bread, and drink the wine which I have mingled." They were partaking with Him, the bread representing His body and the wine representing His blood. The Holy Spirit (wine) along with His Father (bread) was in Him as a part of His body and His blood. When we partake of Holy Communion, we are partaking of the

Father, Son and Holy Spirit. It is another agreement between heaven and earth, for them to dwell within us, by receiving them through the bread and the fruit of the vine. "For *in Him* dwelleth *all* *the fullness* of the Godhead bodily" (Col. 2:9).

Jesus and His Heavenly Father were complete when they were joined by His Heavenly Mother—the three in one, united together on earth. His first miracle was a reflection between heaven and earth, when He followed His earthly mother's instructions and turned water into wine, at the wedding feast in Cana, signifying His Heavenly Mother's influence, in giving Him the power for ministry in the miracle department. His earthly mother being instrumental in the beginning of His ministry, by instructing Him to change the water into wine, was an agreement on earth for His Heavenly Mother to release the power of the Holy Spirit—*the new wine*—in Him for ministry; following His water baptism by John with the baptism of the Holy Spirit—appearing in the form of a Dove at the river Jordan.

Wisdom and understanding are clearly referred to in scripture, as She and Her. "Hear, O Israel: The Lord our God is one Lord" (Deut. 6:4). This does not mean that God is limited to being one or the other, why would God have referred to being in the Image of both male and female, if either part were to be discounted or considered a lesser being? There is no caste system in the Kingdom of God. Jesus said the Comforter would lead us into all truth, and who but *Wisdom* would have the *understanding* to be *capable of leading us into all truth*? Wisdom speaking in Proverbs declares: "For my mouth shall speak truth; and wickedness is an abomination to my lips... For whoso findeth me findeth *life*, [Life in the Tree of Life] and shall find favor of the Lord. But he that sinneth against me **wrongeth his own soul;** All they that hate me love death" [The corruptible seed in man] (Prov. 8:7.35.36).

Have you ever known of a birth without the presence of a birth mother? How can one be born again without a birthing mother? Jesus, born of the Spirit on earth to an earthly mother through a natural birth; made preparation through agreements and covenants with man to bring the Mother of all creation to earth disguised as the Holy Spirit, to birth a new creation in man by awakening us to our true identity, through an Immaculate Conception. She was released from His side when it was pierced—as Eve was released from Adam's side. It appears that it was necessary that His Heavenly Mother be released from His side by—a mortal man of authority—a soldier who unknowingly was giving permission for Her to be released to dwell among us. Another thought to consider is: Eve being released from Adam's side was instrumental in separating man from God. The Holy Spirit, released from Jesus's side is here to be instrumental in reconciling man to God by a rebirth, through the power of *Grace, Truth, Mercy* and *Love.*

She could not freely dwell among or within men on earth, until the final atonement for sin was complete. She was limited to Jesus until He ascended and offered His shed blood upon the Mercy Seat—then She, like the Father has been limited in operation by man's invitation and acceptance of Her—which first occurred in the upper room on the day of Pentecost, and most likely then because Her identity was concealed, just as *our true identity has been veiled* until the fullness of time—the time for the restitution of all things in heaven and in earth. "That in the dispensation of the fullness of times He might gather together *in one* all things in Christ, *both which are in heaven and which are on earth*; even in Him" (Eph. 1:10). What have we failed to acknowledge concerning heaven that is seen on earth? Where does our faith need to be applied to bring heaven and earth together in perfect alignment? What is the missing link? To bring heaven and earth together in perfect alignment, it is necessary that there be a picture perfect reflection, between heaven and earth. This can only be accomplished when the whole truth concerning *the complete family in heaven,* is accepted and received on earth. "Thy Kingdom come, thy will be done in earth **as** *it is **in*** heaven" (Matt. 6:10).

The Old Testament is filled with types and shadows and agreements with covenants—preparing for Jesus to come to earth as God concealed and disguised in the flesh. Our Heavenly Mother had to come to earth in the Spirit—as the Holy Spirit—concealing Her identity, to be received and concealed in our flesh. Just as it was necessary that Jacob disguise himself as Esau, to prepare the way for Jesus to come to earth disguised as a natural man—Jesus receiving the Holy Spirit into the earth at His baptism, leveled the way for His Holy Mother to enter the earth disguised as the Holy Spirit. She also had to be received in type on earth, through John the beloved's acceptance of Jesus's earthly mother—inviting her to dwell with him in *his own home*—producing an agreement to make it legal: an example of God always doing things decently and in order and not overriding man's will.

Jesus, received His Heavenly Mother into the earth realm, at His baptism, concealed in the form of a Dove. When He received Her to dwell in Him—She was able to benefit from all of the covenants and agreements for Him to be on the earth.

Even though She was able to, enter the earth realm through covenants God made with man for Jesus to be on earth, to welcome Her into Himself—there were agreements and covenants pertaining to Her exclusively that were necessary to seal the deal—for Her to legally be here—such as the acceptance, concerning Jesus's earthly mother, through John. Man also had to choose to receive Her in the Person of the Holy Spirit, by following Jesus's instructions to wait in the upper room for Her to appear.

After Jesus told His disciples to wait for another Comforter, in the same conversation, He also told them: "I have many things to say to you, but ye cannot bear them now" (John 16:12). He could very well have been speaking of the gender of the one He was sending to them. Hopefully, those who are still reading this book can bear to hear it now.

> Supple as the willow tree,
> Whose branches catch the wind,
> Holiness can dance in thee,
> And gather children in.
>
> Mightiness and innocence,
> Entwine their simple leaves,
> Where Wisdom, in the fear of God,
> Spreads fragrances, of peace.
>
> Sheltered by the canopy,
> The counsel of the Lord,
> Entered in, by peace to rest,
> Holds one safely to His breast

Deepest intuition walks,
Where reason never trod,
And comprehends maternity,
The feminine—counterpart of God.

Summary: Every aspect of Jesus's earthly existence contained a spiritual significance. Beginning with being born on earth to a natural mother—who represented His Heavenly Mother. At His baptism receiving the Holy Spirit—His Heavenly Mother in the likeness of a Dove. Going into a geographical wilderness—to experience a spiritual wilderness of temptation by the adversary of our souls. At the wedding in Cana, in obedience to His mother's request—changing water into wine, signifying the water from which we are born on this earth, from the womb of the mother that birthed us, to being changed by a rebirth—when we are born through an Immaculate Conception by the Holy Spirit. Opening the eyes of the blind and ears of the deaf—making the lame to walk signifying—having our eyes and ears of understanding opened so that we can walk in the Spirit, no longer lamely stumbling in the darkness of this natural world.

Chapter Fourteen

Holy Mother

Some may wonder what difference it makes whether the Holy Spirit is a He, She or It, and what it has to do with anything. Since it seems to matter that we who inhabit the earth, which is a reflection of what is in heaven—are male and female and since the invisible things of creation are clearly seen by things that are made; it is really simple to see that there can't be one without the other to reflect it. The only likeness spoken of in the New Testament, for the Holy Spirit is the likeness of a Dove. We should in no wise limit the earthly form of the Holy Spirit to be that of a fowl of the air.

The whole idea of the Holy Spirit having an identity that is lesser than that of the Father and the Son is very unlikely. In the light of Jesus's own words: "in earth as it is in heaven," without representation in heaven, the female species would be illegal inhabitants on earth. There would be no other option than for there to be three males making up the *eternal power and Godhead,* or two males and an it of some sort—since the invisible things of heaven are clearly seen by the things on earth that are made—if either of these options were true, from where did the *pattern* for Eve originate and *who* in heaven *is she* a reflection of?

It appears to be important for us to know that we have a Father (He) in heaven, as is reflected on earth by earthly fathers, and it is extremely important to understand that our Heavenly Father has a Son, who is His Express Image and that Image is reproduced in us by the Holy Spirit whom Jesus sent to be our Comforter—as a *mother* comforts her children. "As one whom his *mother* comforteth, so will I comfort you" (Is. 66:13).

Having a Heavenly Mother, as well as a Father and Brother should not be a matter of controversy. Any reaction to the contrary would be contrary to the very laws of nature where male + female=seed after their own kind—even plants and animals are governed by the same laws of nature. No need to sit on the fence—nothing else makes sense. There are many single parents in the world today. Could it be because there is a lack of faith and acceptance on earth in a complete family in heaven?

Since most of our earthly mother's occupy a special place in our hearts, our Heavenly Mother should occupy a special place as well. One thing the majority of males have in common is a defensive, protective caring for their mothers. Jesus's own red letter words are an example: "Wherefore I say unto you, all manner of sin and blasphemy shall be forgiven unto men: And whosoever speaketh a word against the Son of man, it shall be forgiven him: but whosoever speaketh a word against the Holy Ghost, it shall not be forgiven him, neither in this world, or either in the *world* to come" (Matt. 12:31.32). Sounds very much like a son who loves and honors his mother. The only one who would speak a word against the Holy Ghost is the man of sin that sits in our temple, claiming to be us. *We are victims of identity theft*—a reflection between the invisible heavenly realm and what is going on in the earth today that is clearly reflecting it.

Within our lump of clay dwells our true identity that cannot sin. There are those who may have wondered what the following scripture means, since all have sinned. "Whosoever is born of God doth not commit sin; for His Seed remaineth in him; and he cannot sin, because he is born of God. In this the children of God are manifest, [the Seed of the Image of God that does not sin] and the children of the devil; [spawned by the man of sin], whosoever doeth not righteousness is not of God, neither he that loveth not his brother" (I John 3:9.10). This is speaking of the intruder that is a parasite attached to our lump of clay—an example of the necessity of rightly dividing the Word of Truth.

Our true identity, as the Seed of the Image of God, is the one that cannot sin and would never blaspheme the Son of Man or the Holy Ghost. Our salvation does not rest with the dishonor of the man of sin—the parasite in our lump of clay that claims to be us—a usurper that stole the dominion from Adam and Eve, putting us all in bondage.

When Rebekah brought meat she had prepared for Isaac so that Jacob could give it to him, Isaac asked how he found the meat so quickly, Jacob replied: *"because the Lord thy God brought it to me"* (Gen.27:20). Rebekah, acting in God's stead, was in type reflecting our Heavenly Mother, as an obedient daughter. Jacob was submitting to his mother as unto the Lord. Jesus, like Jacob before Him, submitted to His mother's instruction, by turning the water into wine at the wedding feast in Cana. In like manner we are to submit to the guidance and leading of the Holy Spirit.

In the Song of Deborah, found in the book of Judges, she declared herself a Mother in Israel. "The inhabitants of the villages ceased, they ceased in Israel, until that I Deborah arose—a Mother in Israel" (Judges 5:7). Another reflection of the pattern in heaven—for females to exist on earth. It is time for *all of Her children* to rise up and call Her blessed.

The Catholic faith is known for its veneration of Jesus's earthly mother—the Virgin Mary, they alone have fulfilled the words spoken by Mary that all generations would call her blessed—giving life to her words from generation to generation by referring to her as the Blessed Virgin. "And Mary said: My soul doth magnify the Lord, And my spirit hath rejoiced in God my Savior. For He hath regarded the lowly estate of His handmaiden: for, behold, from henceforth all generations shall call me blessed" (Luke 1:46-48). If not for their faithful dedication to honor the Blessed Virgin, she would most likely be allocated to honorable mention in Christmas and Easter Pageants.

The veneration of Jesus's earthly mother has been an important faith agreement in the reflection between heaven and earth—the blessing of His earthly mother has been appropriated in the heavenly realm. Nuns in the Catholic faith, being presided over by a Mother Superior is another reflection of the Heavenly Mother on earth. The reason it is those of the Catholic faith, who have visions of what they believe to be the Virgin Mary is: what we believe and what we can receive from God has a lot to do with what we are open to receive. They have been taught to honor the Blessed Virgin and are the ones with the faith to see such apparitions.

Bernadette Soubirous, had visions of one she referred to as a Beautiful Lady. When it was suggested to her that it was a vision of the Virgin Mary, like the statues in the Church, she denied it and said it was not like the statues of the Virgin in the Church. When the Lady was asked by Bernadette what her name was She replied: "I am the Immaculate Conception." It is through the Holy Spirit, bringing life to the Seed of God that has lain dormant in man, that we can be rebirthed as Jesus was birthed—He came to reveal the existence of our *true identity*, born of God through an Immaculate Conception.

The Beautiful Lady of Bernadette's vision—who was very likely, an apparition of the Great Wonder in heaven—yet to be fully recognized on earth—led her to discover a healing spring in Lourdes France. Her vision occurred in Massabielle, where the refuse of *rotting flesh* from the hospital was burned outside the city. The Holy Spirit—Mother of us all is the Life of the healing spring contained within the Seed of the Image of God that resides in mankind as our *true identity*. She consumes the refuse of *our rotting flesh* as well, with the fire of Her Holy presence within us; but only with our permission—at our invitation and our desire to be cleansed from unrighteousness.

"I lead in the way of righteousness, in the *midst of the paths of judgment*: that I may cause those that love me to inherit substance; and I will fill their treasures. The Lord possessed me in the beginning of His way, before His works of old. I was set up from everlasting from the beginning, or ever the earth was" (Prov. 8:20-22). These words were spoken by the Spirit of Wisdom—that has been accurately translated as She.

She leads Her Seed, the Seed of the Woman that bruises the serpents head, in the way of righteousness, in the *midst of the paths of judgment,* because the natural man *dwells* in the path of judgment. The two-edged sword of the Lord rightly divides man by the Word of the Lord, by separating the seed of the natural man—from the soul of man. The soul cannot exist without a Spirit—to exist on earth there has to be a body for the soul and Spirit to dwell in. Without the body the Spirit and soul *lose their visibility, but not their reality.*

> No one living ever dies,
> For deep within the soul their lies
> The source of life that cannot stay,
> Beneath the earth confined to clay.
>
> Silently as raindrops leave,
> Earth majestically to weave,
> Clouds that sail in sunlit skies,
> No one living ever dies.
>
> The Breath of God that forms the soul,
> The spark of life we now behold,
> Losing visibility, loses no reality,
> But must break forth and must arise,
> For no one living ever dies.

"And as we have borne the image of the earthly, we shall also bear the image of the heavenly. Behold I show you a mystery; we shall not all sleep, but we shall all be changed in a moment in the twinkling of an eye… So when this corruptible shall have put on incorruption, and this mortal shall have put on immortality, *then* shall be brought to pass the saying that is written, *Death is swallowed up in victory*" (I Cor. 15:49.51.52.54).

Representing man, born in sin unto death; Jesus put death-to-death on the Cross. It is extremely important that we visualize ourselves on the Cross with Him and reckon ourselves to be dead to sin. Likewise reckon ye also yourselves to be dead indeed unto sin, but alive unto God through Jesus Christ our Lord" (Rom. 6:11). It is only by mistaken identity and misdirected faith that has taken us on a detour from the truth, that we believe ourselves to be sinners. We are held captive by sin, and are deceived by the man of sin—causing us to err. The old adage: the devil made me do it, is not far from the truth.

"As a man thinketh in his heart so is he" (Prov. 23:7). God has dealt to every man the measure of faith. Faith is a powerful part of us and can operate for or against us, depending on what we believe. "According to your faith be it unto you" (Matt. 10:29). Jesus did not fail. He carried our sin, diseases and all of the curses the natural man is subject to and put them to death on the Cross. We need not carry any of that baggage ourselves. The natural man being *terminated,* on the Cross can only exist in the illusion, perpetrated by the belief in its existence, through a lack of understanding of the finished work of the Cross, and being unaware of our true heritage. The fact that we have not fully appropriated the finished work of the Cross doesn't make it any less true. The Cross was the end of an age and the resurrection was the beginning of a new era entirely, ushering us into the *dispensation* of the Holy Spirit. The *reality* of the truth can only be realized by the work of the Holy Spirit in each individual.

"And there appeared *a great wonder in heaven*; a woman clothed with the sun and the *moon under her feet,* and upon her head a crown of twelve stars. [The great wonder is said to be seen in heaven; She is not said to be seen on earth—She is *a mystery on earth*]. And there appeared another wonder in heaven; and behold a great red dragon… And the dragon was wroth with the woman, and went to make war with the remnant of *Her Seed,* which keep the commandments of God and have the testimony of Jesus Christ" (Rev. 12:1.3.17).

> An ancient, but new thing is in the earth,
> One that will soon be brought to birth.
> Crowned with Stars and clothed with the Sun,
> Ready for the battle that must be won.
>
> She stands with the Moon beneath Her feet,
> As the great red dragon—She's prepared to meet.
> The Seed of the Woman wounds his head,
> As the remnant of Her Seed, by Christ are led.
>
> In righteousness and holiness, they do stand,
> Eager to obey, they await His command.
> With the Fire of Love from the Mercy Seat
> Our Lady among us—makes us complete.

The Mother of the Godhead *needs to be accepted* and received in the earth, as Mother of us all, as in the days of the "voice of the seventh angel, when He shall begin to sound, the mystery of God should be finished" (Rev.10:7), "And the seventh angel sounded; and there were great voices in heaven saying, the kingdoms of this world are become the Kingdom's of our Lord and of His Christ..." (Rev. 11:15). *The mystery of God*—unsealed—is our Holy Mother revealed.

> Encompass us Holy Spirit with your love,
> Truth, in likeness of a Dove—concealed,
> The Mystery of God, is now unsealed,
> As our Holy Mother is revealed.

Another thought to consider is: the Spirit of the Father was able to dwell on earth in the physical form of Jesus, who unlike Adam remained sinless and became the Father's abode—receiving His Mother back into the earth at His baptism—He replicated Adam's containing the female, before she was separated from his side. The union of Adam and Eve produced after their likeness, a seed of sin and a Seed of God. The Holy Spirit was separated from Jesus side, at His death for the purpose of gathering together all of the dividends produced from the original creation that went awry—through an Immaculate Conception creating a new man by awakening us to the awareness of God's Seed within us—uniting heaven and earth as one, a definite witness to God's declaring the end from the beginning. "Declaring the end from the beginning, and from ancient times the *things*, that are not *yet* done saying *my counsel shall stand*, and I will do all my pleasure" (Is. 46:10). He had a purpose in the beginning, from ancient times, that will stand, and the things not yet done—because sin entered the world will not prevent His ultimate purpose. He will simply *gather His chosen Seed*, hidden in every man—finishing what He started— completing His remarkable plan.

"And I will put enmity between thee and the woman, and between thy seed and Her Seed, it shall bruise thy head, and thou shalt bruise his heel" (Gen. 3:15). The deceiver in the garden was well aware of the importance concerning the woman's Seed. That is why he was determined to intercept it.

The serpent wanted to produce a seed of disobedience through Adam and Eve to keep God's Seed from inheriting the earth. The physical form of man and the earth from which he came was a prize to be desired—a prize the serpent cunningly took through subtlety and deceit. God gave man the *gift* of choice, a gift that the serpent could not take away. "For the gifts and calling of God are without repentance [irrevocable]" (Rom. 11:29). The King's—(God's) seal was clearly stamped on man's choice—as proof of purchase from the beginning.

Jesus bruised the serpents head and *our walk* (heel) has been bruised due to our lack of understanding of the truth concerning our identity and inheritance. It was man's choice that brought condemnation into the world and it has to be man's choice that will bring restoration through reconciliation. The deceiver has had an agenda against the woman since the beginning of creation. The abuse the woman has suffered and the right's she has been denied, as seen throughout history, verifies the agenda the deceiver has perpetrated against woman-kind. That is why she has had to stand firm and fight for every inch of ground she has gained through the ages.

The evidence of her importance is seen throughout the Old Testament accounts of the Seed of promise, that was promised to Abraham through Sarah, and continued through Rebekah, Rachel and even Tamar who had to trick Judah because she was destined to produce the Seed she was being denied. Ruth, a widow, having born no children—through the *guidance* and *direction* of Naomi, her mother-in-law, (a type of the Holy Spirit), Ruth was able to continue the Seed line through Boaz a near kinsman of Elimelech—husband of Naomi. Ruth was destined to carry the Seed that became Obed—the father of Jesse—the father of David. Barren women producing the promised Seed culminated in Mary, a chosen Virgin, giving birth to Jesus—the *Ultimate Seed of Promise.*

The role of chosen women was vital in producing the chosen Seed, the chosen men had other children, but the chosen women were barren until they produced the chosen one. Rebekah's unique purpose was to bear twins to separate the chosen one from the natural one. The Seed of the woman denotes the rebirth of mankind through an Immaculate Conception—by the *true* Mother of our *true* identity—the Holy Spirit.

Jesus, born of a Virgin, was the result of an Immaculate Conception—that resulted in our Spiritual rebirth—by the same manner of conception. When the Seed of the woman is manifested in man-kind through an Immaculate Conception, it bruises the head (dominion) of the seed of disobedience—that was sown by the serpent.

> Jesus brought to birth—by His mother on earth,
> His mission and purpose:
> Shedding His blood—revealing our worth.
> To the Holy Spirit—His Heavenly Mother,
> From His wounded side—He gave birth,
> Through redeeming—atonement,
> Restoring to Her—a place on earth.

Summary: Doubt is the nemesis of faith; it blocks faith and renders it ineffective. Doubt and faith are opposites, we can't operate in one while operating in the other, it is definitely an either or. Death must die for Life to live—for the fruit of Life to freely give—life abundant, pressed down shaken together and running over; producing faith, hope and love, through grace and mercy. We must not *measure* truth by what ourselves or others are able to receive and understand. We are being processed to be conformed to the Image of God beyond our ability to *fully* comprehend, until we come to the full *measure* of Christ Jesus. "Eye hath not seen, nor ear heard, neither have entered into the heart of man, the things which God hath prepared for them that love Him" (I Cor. 2:9).

After God finished the work of creation and entered into His rest, His intention was for man to join Him in His rest; to be His resting partner. The fourth chapter of Hebrews strongly stresses the importance of entering into His rest: "Let us therefore **fear**, lest, a promise being left *us* of entering into His *rest*, any of you should seem to come short of it… For we which have *believed* **do** enter into rest; as I have sworn in my wrath; they shall enter into my rest: *although the works* **were** *finished from the foundation of the world*… Seeing therefore it remaineth that *some must enter therein*, and they to whom it was first preached entered not in because of unbelief" (Heb. 4:1.3.6).

The truth unveiled, reveals the reason the enemy's main purpose is to aggravate, and agitate our souls, using every means available to do so. The primary purpose, being to keep us from the *rest* that was prepared for us from the foundation of the world. A lack of rest in our soul has its basis in *unbelief.*

We are inundated with fears, frustrations, noise pollution and every other means possible to keep our souls agitated.

"For if Jesus had given them rest, then would He not afterward spoken of another day... There remaineth therefore a rest to the people of God... For he that has entered into His rest, he also hath ceased from his own works as God did from His.... Let us labor therefore to enter into that rest, lest any man *fall* after the same example of unbelief" (Heb. 4:8-11). What these scriptures are declaring is the bottom line: if we are not resting, we are not *truly* believing. Jesus did not give them rest because they couldn't enter in due to their unbelief. We are instructed to labor to enter into rest—it is an uphill battle because of the enemy's agenda against our souls reaching the *goal* of entering into rest. **It remaineth that some must enter in.** Labor was never a part of God's plan for us, it was included in the curse that man should work by the sweat of his brow, to sustain himself. This doesn't mean that we are to lie around doing nothing, but all that we do is to be done from a place of peace and rest in our soul. No more aggravation or agitation.

Oh, restless soul,
Don't you know,
Entering rest,
Is the goal?

We are a treasure,
Designed for His pleasure.
Worth without measure,
Body and soul.

Chapter Fifteen

Everlasting Love

A Message from Jesus to His Brothers and Sisters

This is what Jesus was declaring to us Through His many parables:

His blood, shed for us, has washed off all of the labels man has placed on us. "For He is our peace who hath made both one, and hath torn down the middle wall of partition between us…for to make in Himself of twain one new man, so making peace" (Eph. 2:14). It is only us: our Father, His Son, and our Comforter. In reality, we are—as He is. "Herein is our love made perfect, that we may have boldness in the day of judgment: because as He is so are we in this world" (1 John 4:17).

We have been held captive; his blood was shed to remit the sin that is holding us captive, and now sin can only hold us captive in our mind—He came to renew our mind and exchange our thoughts for His thoughts. "For I know the thoughts that

I think toward you, thoughts of peace, and not of evil, to give you an expected end" (Jer. 29:11).

It was spoken of Him: "Thou hast ascended on high, thou hast led captivity captive: thou hast received gifts for men; yea *for* the **rebellious** also, that the Lord God might dwell *among them*. Blessed be the Lord who daily loadeth us with benefits, even the God of our salvation" (Ps. 68:18.19). God's gifts are not withheld because of man's imperfections—He is even willing to put up with our **rebellious** nature just so He can dwell among men; if it were not so He would not be able to dwell among the inhabitants of the earth at all. Through His Seed that dwells in us, we are all *one family*, made up of *all* nations and *all* peoples: *all* loved and *accepted* in the beloved. "In whom we have redemption through His blood; the forgiveness of sin, according to the riches of His grace" (Eph. 1:7). The noise pollution heard on earth, in its multitudinous forms, is purposefully attempting to drown out the still small voice— heard only in quietness—in the very depth of our soul.

Your Father grieves: "Woe is me for my hurt! My wound is grievous; but I said, Truly this *is* a grief, and I must bear it. My tabernacle is spoiled, and my cords are broken; my children are gone forth of me, and they *are* not; *there is* none to stretch my tent anymore, and to set up my curtains" (Jer. 10:19.20).

After dominion was misappropriated, in the beginning of creation, and the bodies seized, our *God was limited* to being *represented* by an Ark surrounded by a tent. The Ark was carried about between two poles for forty years in the wilderness. The cherubim, covering the Ark of the Covenant, were a picture of the cherubim, with *flaming swords*, guarding the Tree of Life.

Noah and his family were spared from destruction, by an ark—his obedience through a ***covenant*** with God to receive instructions for building an ark—provided the necessary agreement on earth granting permission for the Creator of the universe to ***covenant*** with man to build an Ark to *represent* Him—that is why it is called the Ark of the ***Covenant***. How *very sad*—that the God of all creation was made homeless on earth, because of man's choice—until an Ark was built to become the only *habitation* for His Spirit. God was able to *dwell among them*, by *also* like Noah, being spared by an Ark—containing manna that fed His people in the wilderness, a type of Jesus breaking the bread of life with man. Also housed in the Ark were the stone tablets engraved with the ten commandments—*representing* the ***covenant*** God made with Moses—along with Aaron's rod that budded, representing the Holy Spirit, raising the lifeless body of Jesus from the dead. We are all lifeless branches until His resurrection life through an Immaculate Conception of the Holy Spirit buds forth in us.

The Father, Son and Holy Spirit all had representation in the Ark of the Covenant. All of the contents in the Ark provided the necessary agreement for God's Spirit to inhabit the Ark, because the budding rod, the manna and the ten commandments were all representations of God—giving dominion for Him to legally inhabit the Ark. Until His Son was born on earth in a body of flesh the Godhead—the Creator of all things had no flesh to dwell in—because of a covenant man did not keep. Jesus is the new covenant; He has made provision for the Creator of all things, in heaven and earth, to dwell among men, through the Comforter, whom we have received to dwell in our flesh.

His compassions are reserved for His Seed in everyman— His lost sheep. "My sheep wandered through all the mountains, and upon every high hill: yea, my flock was scattered upon all the face of the earth, and none did search or seek *after them*. For thus saith the Lord God; Behold, I, even I, will both search my sheep, and seek them out" (Ez. 34:6.11). He came to search out and shepherd His sheep, by sending the Holy Spirit, to lead them into truth. "I will feed my flock, and I will cause them to lie down, saith the Lord God. I will *seek* that which was lost, and bring again that which was driven away, and will bind up that *which was* broken, and will strengthen that which was sick" (Ez. 34:15.16).

Thousands and thousands of years—He has waited to set the captives free, His Seed, is held captive within the prison *cells* of man, while the human race, unknowingly has *opposed their own souls* and their true identity as children of the Living God. "But this is a people robbed and spoiled; *they are* all of them **snared in holes,** and they are **hid in prison houses**: they are for a prey, and none delivereth; for a spoil, and none saith Restore. Who among you will give ear to this? *who* will harken and hear for the time to come?" (Is. 42:22-23).

The story of Joseph draws a word picture to show the captivity of the Seed of God. He was thrown into a pit, **snared in a hole**, and like the soul, sold into slavery and **hid in a prison house**. "As for thee also, by the blood of the covenant I have sent forth thy prisoners out of the pit wherein *is* no water" (Zech. 9:11). God's Seed is held captive by the seed of the natural man. The soul of man, who still *retains the choice*, must call out for deliverance. God's hands willingly given to the shackles of mankind must be untied by the same hands that tied them—*the choice of man*—then He will be free to intervene and set all of the oppressed captives free. "... to loose the bands of wickedness, to undo the heavy burdens, and to let the oppressed go free, and that ye break every yoke" (Is.58:6).

Jesus on earth, allowed Himself to be put into the hands of man, a reflection between heaven and earth, when the Godhead gave dominion over the earth to man. "Thinkest thou that I cannot now pray to my Father, and He shall presently give me more than twelve legions of angels? But how then shall the scriptures be fulfilled, that *thus it must be*?" (Matt. 26:53.54). The Image of His Father, He also honored His Father's Word by giving Himself over to the will and *choice* of man. Even in His final hour man was given the opportunity to choose Him or Barabbas, a known criminal, to be pardoned and set free. Once again, the *will of the people* prevailed in *choosing against their own souls.* In the days of Samuel the prophet, when the people desired a king to rule over them, Samuel was displeased, and prayed to the Lord. "And the Lord said unto Samuel, harken to the *voice* of the people and *do all* that they *say unto thee,* for they have not rejected thee, but they have rejected me, that I should not reign over them" (I Sam. 8:7).

God submits to the will of the people and will not override the gift of freewill that was given at the beginning of creation. The Creator of man is the only one with the blueprint to guide His creation. "For I know the thoughts that I think toward you thoughts of peace and not of evil, to give you an ***expected end***" (Jer. 29:11). In the world man has created for himself—one never knows what to expect.

Clear and gentle curves of shoreline,
Reach as far as eye can see,
With a haunting, lonely beauty that
Recalls, your warmth to me.

Like the regal strength of waters,
Rolling inward from the sea,
Come, Eternal Father,
Come returning, come to me.

In a realm beyond my knowing,
Lies a hidden memory,
Where a child, adoring,
Sits upon a Father's knee.

Now I sit and watch the breakers
Of the water from the sea,
And my heart, which cries for mending,
Calls, "My Father, come to me."

As the waves repeated rhythm,
Plays a searching melody,
My soul begins its singing
For your presence, like the sea.

Motivated by the Moon's pull,
Drawn by forces man can't see,
"Come my dear Eternal Father,
With the Morning Star to me."

Your Mother weeps: "Thus saith the Lord: a voice was heard in Ra-mah, lamentation and bitter weeping. Rachel weeping for her children, refused to be comforted for her children, because they *were* not. "Arise, cry out in the night: in the beginning of the watches pour out thine heart like water, before the face of the Lord; lift up thy hands toward Him for the *life* of thy young children, that faint for hunger in the top of every street...those that I have swaddled and brought up hath mine enemies consumed" (Lam. 2:19.22). "There is none to guide Her among all the sons *whom* she brought forth; neither is *there one* that taketh Her by the hand of all the sons that she hath brought up...by whom shall I comfort thee? Thy sons have fainted, they lie at the head of all the streets"...(Is. 51:18-20). These scriptures are referring to the lost sheep—the Chosen Seed of God, that has been held captive within man—the Spiritual lineage of Jacob-Israel—of which natural Israel is a type. Thus saith the Lord; refrain thy voice from weeping, and thine eyes from tears; for thy work shall be rewarded saith the Lord; and they shall come again from the land of the enemy, and there is hope in their end, saith the Lord, that thy children shall come again to their own border" (Jer. 31:15-17). Natural Israel becoming a state in 1948—is a *parable* and a *type* of the Holy Seed, born of God, rising up and taking back our land. A natural action producing a spiritual agreement for the Seed of God within us to reclaim the land, (*our bodies*) as well as all of the lost aspects of dominion that rightfully belong to us—that was misappropriated in the beginning.

"For the Lord hath redeemed Jacob, and ransomed him from the hand of *him that* was stronger than he" (Jer. 31: 11). "Yea, I have loved thee with an everlasting love; therefore with loving kindness have I drawn thee. For thus saith the Lord; sing with gladness for Jacob, and shout among the chief of the nations: *publish ye*, praise me, and say **O Lord save thy people, the remnant of Israel**" (Jer. 31:3.7). God's Seed *hidden* in every one of us is the *remnant*, awaiting the sound of the trumpet. "Awake, awake, put on strength, O arm of the Lord; awake, as in the ancient days, in the generations of old" (Is. 51:9). "Arise shine, for thy light is come, and the glory of the Lord, is risen upon thee" (Is. 60:1). "But this shall be the covenant that I will make with the house of Israel; after those days, saith the Lord, *I will put* my law in their inward parts, and write it in their hearts and will be their God and they shall be my people. And they shall teach no more every man his neighbor, and every man his brother saying, know the Lord; for **they shall all know me,** from the least of them to the greatest of them, saith the Lord; for I will forgive their iniquity, and I will remember their sin no more" (Jer. 31:33.34).

The plea:
Who are you, Lady of gentlest eyes?"
Beneath my confusion, in peace, you reside
I know you; in silence, I hear you reply,
Faithful to God, while selfish I fly.
I need you—please help me—my world is awry
I know you would live this life—far better than I.

The reply:
"Simply I'm waiting unable to rise,
Till flesh has surrendered, cast off its disguise.
Your eyes will be opened,

When your heart has grown wise.
You will find, I am truth and the rest is all lies.
Abide in the Life that the Father supplies,
I will be here, when the morning arrives."

The disciples were asked to wait in an upper room for the Comforter to come—to be welcomed into the earth. The Comforter is here, in the measure She has been received, by concealing Her identity in the Holy Spirit. She has been welcomed as Comforter and Holy Spirit; for Her to birth the Kingdom of God, *She needs to be accepted and welcomed as Mother.* "Before she travailed, she brought forth; before her pain came she was delivered of a man child. Who hath heard such a thing? Who hath seen such things? Shall the earth be made to bring forth in one day? *or* shall a nation be born at once? For as soon as Zion travailed, she brought forth her children. [Her Seed in each of us] Shall I bring to birth, and not cause to bring forth? Saith the Lord: shall I cause to bring forth, and shut *the womb*? Saith God. As one whom **his mother comforteth,** so will I comfort you" (Is. 66:7-8.9.12.13). This scripture is referring to the Spiritual Jerusalem of which *we are all a part.* It can also be applied to the natural Jerusalem, as a type and reflection. **There can never be a birth, without a birth mother.** The Kingdom of God is brought to birth by the "New Jerusalem Mother of us all." May She no longer remain barren and bereft of Her children—but as a fruitful bough, may She be released through faith and the acceptance of mankind, to bear much fruit in the earth—bringing forth the Seed of the Image of God within us, through an Immaculate Conception.

"Behold I show you a mystery; we shall not all sleep, but we shall all be changed. In a moment, in the twinkling of an eye, at the last trump: for the trumpet shall sound, and the dead shall be raised *incorruptible,* and we shall be changed. For this *corruptible* **must** *put on incorruption,* and this mortal **must** put on *immortality*… then shall be brought to pass the saying that is written, **death is swallowed up in Victory**" (I Cor. 15:51-54). "Let us search and try our ways, and turn again to the Lord. Let us lift up our heart with *our* hands unto God in the heavens… *and turn again to the Lord"* (Lam. 3:40-41).

He has reconciled us to our Father and our Mother. "… Be ye reconciled to God" (II Cor. 5:20). "Therefore if any man *be* in Christ, *he is* a new creature: old things are passed away; behold; all things are become new. And all things *are* of God, who hath *reconciled* us to Himself by Jesus Christ, and hath given to us the ministry of reconciliation: To wit, that **God was in Christ reconciling the world** unto Himself, **not imputing their trespasses unto them;** and hath *committed unto us* the word of *reconciliation"* (II Cor. 5:17-19). We are to be ambassadors of reconciliation to one another, and *not* ambassadors of judgment that produces condemnation—that leads to degradation.

"Father, the hour is come; glorify thy Son, that thy Son also may glorify thee… As thou hast sent me into the world, even so have I also sent them into the world. And for their sakes I sanctify myself, that they also might be sanctified through the truth. Neither pray I for these alone, but for them also which shall believe on me through their word; **That they all may be one** as thou Father *art* in me, and I in thee, that they also may be one in us: that the world may believe that thou hast sent me. And the glory which thou gavest me I have given them; that they may be one, even as we are one: I in them, and thou in me, that they may be made perfect in one; and that the world may know that thou hast sent me, and *hast loved them, as thou hast loved me*" (John 17:1.18-23).

Come as one—come all
Ransomed from the fall,
Eternal invitation—answer the call
Gather as one—gather all.

Bending low to the earth,
With outstretched wings,
Enter the shelter—the Comforter brings
Welcome as one—welcome all.

"O Jerusalem... how often I would have gathered thy children together, even as a hen gathereth *her* chickens under *her* wings, and ye would not" (Matt. 23:37).

Synopsis

The Holy Bible is the only book in existence that contains so many levels of meaning. If it were possible to calculate each religious order, sect and organization since the beginning of time, that has made the claim to be biblically correct in their doctrine, it would be astonishing, because the *varied interpretations* of the Word of God are numerous, and none are exactly the same.

The Old Testament is *amazingly diverse* in the levels and facets of meaning to be conveyed. A phenomenal aspect of the Word of God is the multiplicity of *parables* throughout the Old Testament that on one level appears *only* to be a historical account. Parables preparing the way for Jesus to enter the earth are the most prevalent. Jesus's main method of teaching was, through the use of parables. He, who came in the Image of His Father, was continuing in the same pattern of communication, to prepare the way for the coming of the Holy Spirit. Among the many levels and facets of the Word, to be gleaned: there is the literal historical—types and shadows—parables—and hidden depths of truth that can *only be discerned* by revelation through the Holy Spirit leading us into the whole truth and nothing but the truth.

Whoever we are and whatever level of understanding we have through our individual walk and experience, the Word of God fits every situation we encounter. The Word goes with us wherever we are, and we can never get beyond its reach. As stated in the poem in Part one, chapter one of this book:

> The Spirit and the Word always agree,
> Yet—with limited vision—we are unable to see,
> The vast hidden treasure concealed therein.
> Seeing through a glass darkly—now unveiled,
> As understanding increases, illuminated from within,
>
> With the dawning of Truth we comprehend,
> The Word of Truth—ever expanding,
> Never ceases to outdistance our finite understanding.
> Its height, depth and breadth, we can never outgrow,
> It is only when we are known—then we will know.

The Old Testament message, while being a literal historical account of mankind from the beginning of creation, is also basically a parable of mankind and God's plan of the ages for man—to restore what was lost, and undo what *man's recreation* has done to God's original creation.

"For behold, I create new heavens and a new earth: and the former shall not be remembered, nor come into mind. But be ye glad and rejoice forever in *that* which I create: for behold, I create Jerusalem a rejoicing and **Her** people a joy" [this is speaking of *all of us* as a part of the New Jerusalem—Mother of us all] (Is. 65:17.18).

A witness to this scripture in Isaiah can be seen, in Revelation chapter 21: 1-3. "And I saw a new heaven and a new earth: for the first heaven and the first earth were passed away: and there was no more sea [division]. And I John saw the holy city, New Jerusalem, **coming down** from God out of heaven, *prepared as a bride adorned for her husband*; And I heard a great voice out of heaven saying, Behold, the tabernacle of God *is* with men, and He will **dwell** with them, and they shall be His people, and God Himself shall be with them, and be their God."

Just as I Corinthians 15: 51-52, states: "… but we shall *all* be changed. In a moment, in the twinkling of an eye, at the last trump…" Not only will we be changed, but heaven and earth will be united as one. The New Jerusalem *coming* **down** from God out of heaven will drape the earth with all that was contained in the original creation—adorning the earth like a bride adorned for her husband, the two becoming one. "But there went up a mist from the earth, and watered the whole face of the ground" (Gen. 2: 6). Like a mist settling upon the earth, it will be clothed with all the beauty and glory of the original Garden. And we will all be changed and mirror the change, just as Adam and Eve mirrored the Garden of Eden, and then mirrored their *own creation* of thorns and thistles. We will all mirror the beauty of Gods New Creation, first within us and then reflected all around us. As it was in the *beginning*, so shall it be from everlasting to everlasting, *world without end*.

"Remember the former things of old: for I am God and there is none else; I am God and *there is none like me*, Declaring the end from the beginning, and from ancient times the things, that are not yet done, saying My counsel shall stand, and I will do all my pleasure" (Is.46: 9.10). "And He that sat upon the throne said, Behold I make all things new. And He said unto me, *Write*: for these words are true and faithful. And He said unto me, **It is done.** I am *Alpha* and *Omega* the **beginning** and the **end**" (Rev. 21:5.6). What *began* in a garden (Eden)—*ended* in a garden (Gethsemane). What *began* on a tree—was *ended* on a tree. What *resulted* in a tomb—was *ended* in a tomb. What began in man and woman (iniquity)—*must end* in man and woman—by the Spirit of life in Christ Jesus making us free from the law of sin and death. **The end** *declared*—*from the beginning.*

Holy Spirit, gentle hand in all we love,
Creating in us more than we've had knowledge of,
Precious Lord, we look in wonder at the skill,
Of the stitches—in the fabric of your will.

It is your hand that guides the needle, we're the thread.
Passing narrowly through places where we are led.
Random stitches—forming shapes we can't discern.
Take on meaning when our souls begin to learn.

Handiwork, designed in your pure heart,
In a pattern so perfect—a priceless work of art,
A communion that is Holy, we now can see,
Among our souls—cross stitched together unto thee.

The above poem ending with the words—"cross stitched together unto thee"—contains a dual message. A type and parable—comparing us to fabric—revealing God's design being created in us; like cross stitching—creating a design on fabric. There is a literal message that can be seen in *the Cross of Jesus*—stitching us together—making us one in Him. "For we know that the *whole* creation groaneth and travaileth in pain together until now...even we ourselves groan within ourselves waiting for the adoption, *to wit*, the redemption of the body" (Rom. 8:22. 23).

The redemption of the body is a subject that has too long been ignored. It is an example of "seeing, is believing"— believing only what we can see—bodies subject to death. What the natural man can see is what he can believe. "As he [man] thinketh in his heart so is he…" (Prov. 23:7). "…*Faith* is the substance of things *hoped* for and the *evidence* of things **not seen**" (Heb. 11:1). As people of faith, it is important that we focus our attention on the completion of redemption—the *vision of **all**—including* the redemption of the body.

Abel, was the Seed of God, and could not remain on earth in his earthly body, due to the dominion of the body being lost, through subtly and deceit—that produced disobedience in His parents. Jesus as the Seed of God, being received into heaven, (invisible realm) chose to offer His earthen vessel. He willingly shed His earthly body—giving up the ghost, to save the soul, by applying His blood on the Mercy Seat. Mary giving birth to Jesus in an earthen vessel is a type and shadow of our Heavenly Mother—redeeming the body through a rebirth, for God's Seed to once more visibly inhabit the earth—when the dominion of the body—is restored to the rightful owner in each one of us.

"Another parable spake He unto them: the Kingdom of God [the Seed of God within us] *is like* unto leaven, which **a woman** took and hid in three measures of meal, [Spirit, soul and body] till the whole was leavened" (Matt. 13:33). God's Seed is a treasure hidden within our earthly body—being brought to birth by the power of the Holy Spirit. Jesus brought redemption to our souls two thousand years ago, fulfilling His commission, when—He said—"***It is finished***: and he bowed His head, and gave up the ghost" (John 19:30). He sent the Holy Spirit to comfort us and lead us into all truth—to complete the plan of God, by dwelling within us, until our whole lump is leavened—bringing redemption to the body—"For with God nothing shall be impossible" (Luke 1:37). "Jesus said unto him, If thou canst believe, all things are possible to him that believeth" (Mark 9:23)..."Go thy way; and as thou hast believed, so be it done unto thee (Matt. 8:13).

Jesus purchased the redemption of our souls—uniting us as one in Him. He sent the Holy Spirit to complete God's remarkable plan for man—to lead us into all truth. The treasure we contain is, a "Pearl of Great Price" (Matt. 13:46). A treasure, created for His pleasure—whose worth cannot be measured—both the *soul* <u>and</u> the *body* that contains it.

"Therefore leaving the principles of the doctrine of Christ, *let us go on unto perfection*: not laying again the foundation of repentance from dead works, and of faith toward God, of the doctrine of baptisms and of laying on of hands, and of resurrection of the dead, and of eternal judgment. And ***this will we do, if God permit***" (Heb. 6:1). "Jesus saith unto her, I am the resurrection and ***the life***; he that *believeth* in Me *though* he were dead, *yet* shall he live; and whosoever ***liveth*** and believeth in Me ***shall never die***. *Believest thou this?*" (John 11: 25.26). Both of these scriptures tell a tale:—revealing how we are seriously lacking in what we are receiving, due to the limitations we place on what we think God will and will not do or can and cannot do. The time is long overdue for us to ***let God be God*** in ***all*** in the earth—as He is in heaven, where He reigns supreme—both male and female.

While man has been replenishing the earth from the beginning of creation, until this present time, the heavens are being populated, paralleling the earth, "…as in heaven so in earth" (Luke 11:2). The Seed of the Image of God and the soul brought forth in the flesh by the breath of God, first in Abel, who was received back into the invisible realm of heaven to await the day of resurrection—his blood crying out from the ground, until it was justified through Jesus Christ, whose blood flowed upon the earth from the Cross—bringing redemption to man and justice for Abel, granting us the ability to live in freedom with liberty and justice: (equity-honor-fairness) for all.

"For what saith the scripture? Abraham believed God and it was counted unto him for righteousness. Who against *hope* believed in *hope*, that he might become the father of many nations, according to that which was spoken, so shall thy Seed be: (Rom. 4:3.18). "Then Abraham gave up the ghost in a good old age, an old man, and full of years; and was gathered to his people" (Gen. 25:8). He was gathered to his people who had gone before him, whose souls were populating the heavens along with all souls containing the Seed of the Image of God, who are awaiting the fullness of time, when the wall of partition that separates us is torn down—joining heaven and earth in union as one.

> Heaven and earth are longing to be woven together as one.
> Threads of a lovely garment, in the hands of the Holy One.
> Weaving our souls together, leaving the fragments behind.
> Completing an elegant garment, woven in His design.

"For He is our peace, who hath made both one, and hath broken down the middle wall of partition between us; Having abolished in His flesh the enmity, [between heaven and earth—between the Seed of His Image, and the soul of man] even the law of commandments contained in ordinances; for to make in Himself *of twain* [duality] *one new man*, so making peace; And that He might reconcile *both* unto God in **one body** by the Cross, having slain the enmity thereby" (Eph. 2:14).

This scripture contains more than one level of interpretation. As our understanding increases we become aware of facets revealed in the Word of God—comparable to facets in a diamond—reflecting various rays of light when illuminated. One facet is the need for reconciliation—man to man—between Jew and Gentile—encompassing all mankind. "So we being many are *one body* in *Christ* and *everyone* members of another" (Rom. 9:2). One facet of meaning does not cancel another. The facet of the Word being illuminated in this book is—the Seed of God united to the soul of man—restoring all that was lost when the soul was deceived into forfeiting dominion to an enemy of *both* God *and* man. "In a moment, in the twinkling of an eye, at the last trump: for the trumpet *shall* sound, and the dead *shall* be changed. For this corruptible *must* put on incorruption, and this mortal *must* put on immortality [uniting heaven and earth—reconciling the Seed of God and the soul of man united as one—the *Cross* having *slain the enmity thereby*]" (I Cor. 15:52.53).

"For we are saved by *hope*; but *hope* that is seen is not *hope*: for what a man seeth, why doth he yet *hope*?" (Rom. 9:24). "Now faith is the substance of things *hoped* for, the evidence of things not seen" (Heb. 11:1). First we must have hope. *Hope* reveals *our desire* to believe, it is the first step toward producing the evidence of faith. Faith is believing—before knowing.

Knowing is when we have eyes to see and ears to hear what doubt can never contest or erase—knowing is *knowing*—that we *know*—that we *know*.

"For now we *know* in part, and we prophesy in part. But when that which is perfect is come, then that which is in part shall be done away...For *now* we see through a glass, darkly; but *then* face to face: now I *know* in part; but then shall I *know* even as also I am *known*. And *now* abideth *faith, hope,* and *charity,* these three; but the greatest of these is charity [love]" (I Cor. 13:10. 12.13).

"Beloved, let us love one another: for love is of God; and every one that loveth is *born of God*, and knoweth God. [His Seed reborn in us] God *is* Love. In this was manifested the love of God toward us, because that God sent His only begotten Son into the world, that we might **live through Him**...Beloved if God so loved us we ought also to *love one another*" (I John 4:9.11).

When we see ourselves through God's eyes—face to face—we will behold Him in each other—reflecting His image—from one to another.

God Was All In One
Containing All of Creation Within Himself

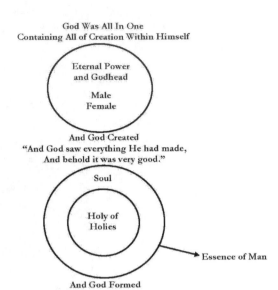

Eternal Power
and Godhead

Male
Female

And God Created
"And God saw everything He had made,
And behold it was very good."

Soul

Holy of
Holies

→ Essence of Man

And God Formed
"Let us make man in our Image"
"And the Lord God formed man of the dust of the ground and breathed into his nostrils the breath of life;
and man became a living soul. And God planted a garden eastward of Eden and there he put the man
whom he had formed."
"And the rib, which the Lord God had taken from man, made He a woman and brought her to the man."

Man
Reconciled to God

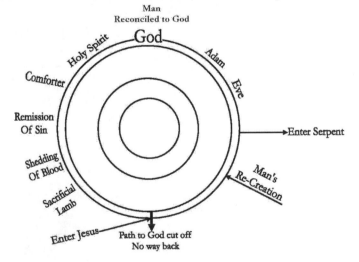

God

Holy Spirit

Adam

Comforter

Eve

Remission
Of Sin

→ Enter Serpent

Shedding
Of Blood

Man's
Re-Creation

Sacrificial
Lamb

Enter Jesus

Path to God cut off
No way back

The Wheat and the Soul

"The Son of Man shall send forth His angels, and they shall gather out of his kingdom all the things that offend, and them which do iniquity" (Matt. 13:41).

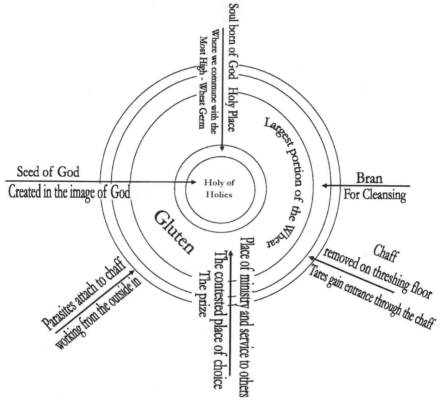

"Whosoever is born of God doth not commit sin; for his seed remaineth in him: and *he cannot sin, because he is born of God*" (1 John 3:9).

207

Bibliography

Illustrated Poem: Adrift, Copyright 1977, Jane Stephens
Art: Wantha Ann Deaton

Chapter One:
Poem: The Spirit and the Word, Copyright 2012, Mary Adams.
Poem: Excerpt from: From the Woman, Copyright 1993, Jane Stephens.

Chapter Two:
Poem: Excerpt from: Pieces and Patches, Copyright 1980, Jane Stephens.

Chapter Three:
Poem: Hannah, Copyright 1980, Jane Stephens
Poem: More than a Stable, Copyright 1995, Mary Adams.

Chapter Four:
Poem: Excerpt from: From the Woman, Copyright 1993, Jane Stephens.
Poem: In His Image, Copyright 2012, Mary Adams.

Chapter Five:
Poem: An Elegant Garment, Copyright 1989, Mary Adams.

Chapter Six:
Poem: Joseph, Copyright 1993, Jane Stephens.

Chapter Seven:
Poem: Excerpt from: Pieces and Patches, Copyright 1980, Jane Stephens.

Chapter Eight:
Poem: The Cleansing Fire, Copyright 1991, Jane Stephens.
Poem: Thank You Lord, Copyright 1982, Jane C Stephens, and Mary Adams.

Chapter Nine:
Illustrated Poem: Small Feet, Copyright 1980, Jane Stephens.
Art: Wantha Ann Deaton.
Poem: Heart Song, Copyright 1991, Jane Stephens, and Mary Adams.
Illustrated Poem: Perfect Love, Copyright 1983, Mary Adams, and 1991 Jane Stephens.
Art: Wantha Ann Deaton

Conclusion:
Poem: The Crucifixion, Copyright 1982, Jane Stephens, and Mary Adams.

Part II

Introduction:
Poem: Draw Me On, Copyright 1977, Jane Stephens

Chapter Ten:
Poem: Excerpt from Poem: Heart Song, Copyright 1991, Jane Stephens and Mary Adams.

Chapter Eleven:
Poem: The Birth of the Kingdom, Copyright 2012, Mary Adams
Poem: Creative Genius, Copyright 2012, Mary Adams

Chapter Twelve:
Poem: Mother of Mercies, Copyright 2012, Mary Adams.
Poem: Heavenly Pattern, Copyright 2011, Mary Adams
Poem: Seed of the Woman, Copyright 2011, Mary Adams

Chapter Thirteen:
Poem: The Willow, Copyright 1991, Jane Stephens.

Chapter Fourteen:

Poem: No One Living Ever Dies, Copyright, 1989, Mary Adams and Jane Stephens.

Poem: Ancient but New, Copyright, 2011, Mary Adams.

Poem: Encompass Us, Copyright, 2012, Mary Adams.

Poem: His Mothers, Copyright 2012, Mary Adams

Poem: Rest, Copyright 2012, Mary Adams

Chapter 15:

Poem: Eternal Father, Copyright 1991, Jane Stephens.

Poem: The Lady, Copyright 1990, Jane Stephens.

Poem: The Gathering, Copyright 2012, Mary Adams.

Synopsis:

Poem: The Spirit and the Word, Copyright 2012, Mary Adams.

Poem: Cross Stitched, Copyright 1990, Jane Stephens and Mary Adams.

Poem: An Elegant Garment, Copyright 1989, Mary Adams.

Illustrated Chart: Creation-the Fall-Reconciliation.

Illustrated Chart: The Wheat and the Soul.

Poems by Jane Stephens: deceased—used by permission of Dr. Michael R. Stephens.

Art work by Wantha Ann Deaton—used by permission of Wantha Ann Deaton.

Acknowledgments

I would like to acknowledge those whose contributions have made this book a reality. I want to thank my family for their help and encouragement. My thanks to those at West Bow Press for their guidance: Madison Lux who worked with me at the beginning, also Sam Fitzgerald and Erin Watson for their help. Special thanks to Mateo Palos, who has guided me through the details leading to completion and production.

I am very grateful for Pastor Jimmy Sowder's contribution in writing the forward for this book and for his enthusiasm as he witnessed to and verified its content through the Word of God written in his heart, as well as through searching the scriptures, while he cheered me onward in the writing.

In Memoriam

I am saddened to add this memoriam to Jimmy Sowder—who arrived on this earth September 1, 1922, and returned to his heavenly Father on November 25, 2012. Even though the loss of Jimmy's presence on earth is heavens gain, he is greatly missed by all of us who love him and treasure the time we had with him. A true man of God. Like David he was a man after God's own heart.

"…The path of the just is as the shining light that shineth more and more unto the perfect day" (Proverbs 4:18).